# PRAISE FOR *P.R.O.S.*

"From the outside looking in, Chris Hope has lived the American dream. But his biggest successes in life have nothing to do with national titles or Super Bowl championships. Chris is a winner because he's learned how to honor God through his life and relationships."

– DAVE RAMSEY,
BESTSELLING AUTHOR AND NATIONALLY
SYNDICATED RADIO SHOW HOST

"I've always admired Chris Hope the football player, but after reading *P.R.O.S.*, my respect for him as a caring human being has gone to an entirely different level! Chris does an incredible job of sharing his many successes as a superstar athlete, but also shows the challenges of his journey as an athlete, a son, a brother, a grandson, a student, etc. The book and life lessons inside of it are stories we can all benefit from hearing. Thank you, Chris, for sharing your story in such open detail and allowing us to learn from your experiences. A must read for ALL!"

– KIRK HERBSTREIT,
ESPN "COLLEGE GAMEDAY" ANALYST

"First of all, I have to commend Chris for his courage, openness, and willingness to take off the Band-Aid of life and reveal the scarred and raw reality that we as professional athletes live. Chris wrote with such honesty and sincerity not often seen, especially when dealing with such a delicate subject as your family. Throughout *P.R.O.S*, Chris strategically and smoothly navigates through life's expectations, experiences, and the decisions that follow a childhood dream of becoming successful, specifically in his case, a professional athlete. Lastly, this book offers clear and precise tools and knowledge that can help develop a roadmap of sorts for not only athletes, but for anyone that aspires to reach and play at the highest level of their profession and will one day be forced to deal with family expectations, society's expectations, and personal expectations."

– JEROME "THE BUS" BETTIS, SUPER BOWL
XL CHAMPION, PRO FOOTBALL HOF (2015)

"This is one of the most enlightening books I've ever read. Chris Hope's willingness to be transparent about the challenges of managing life on and off the field is a priceless tool for any professional. This book is a game changer!"

– BISHOP JOSEPH WALKER, III,
SENIOR PASTOR, MOUNT ZION CHURCH, NASHVILLE

"Chris Hope has been a winner his entire life, and through this exceptional piece of literature, he is offering the real-life, pragmatic, generalizable blueprint for all of us to win in our individual disciplines."

– MYRON L. ROLLE, MD, FOUNDER OF OUR WAY TO
HEALTH, RHODES SCHOLAR

"Chris was known as the Hammer when he played, and it shows in the way he tackles head-on the significance of boundaries with those he loves. This book will rescue families, finances, and futures. Chris' encouraging words show how we can live a life without regrets."

– JOHN MASON,
AUTHOR OF AN ENEMY CALLED AVERAGE

"One of the greatest benefits to my having had a long and enjoyable coaching career is the fact that I have a very large "extended" family in which Chris Hope has long been a part of. Throughout Chris' myriad of messages, many, many people—particularly parents—will find great use in his experiences as they traverse this long and winding road of life."

– DICK LEBEAU,
2X SUPER BOWL CHAMPION(XL, XLIII), HOF 2010

"Chris Hope's success in life on and off the football field after graduating from Florida State doesn't surprise me one bit. He always had his priorities in order. I wish I could say that I played a big part in Chris' success, but it was his upbringing that helped lead to his success."

– BOBBY BOWDEN, FORMER FLORIDA STATE
UNIVERSITY FOOTBALL COACH

"His life's story told in *P.R.O.S.* runs parallel and aligns with his character, demeanor, and personality as a football player and person. One in which he thrived under pressure and shined through adversity without ever losing focus or showing any signs of doubt or fear. If you were a fan of who he was on the football field, after reading this book you will agree with me in saying that *Chris is ten times a better man off the field.* Reading his story will not only inspire and motivate you to achieve, believe, and chase after your own goals and dreams, but provide *hope* that when you accomplish your heart's desires through hard work, faith, and a strong relationship with god. You will not only capture success, but be completely fulfilled with everlasting peace and happiness."

– EDDIE GEORGE, PROFESSIONAL FOOTBALL PLAYER & PROFESSIONAL ACTOR, HEISMAN TROPHY AWARD (1995)

"Chris' courage and love are displayed in this personal account of his struggles with unforeseen adversities on his quest to fulfill his childhood dreams. This book explains very real experiences and emotions in the life of a professional athlete or anyone who is fortunate enough to stumble across success. Chris' life experiences will help young professionals envision and fulfill their goals and teach them how to properly deal with success. His life's experiences are something that so many other athletes are faced with, but Chris gracefully shows how to properly address them in a healthy and fruitful way. Chris' Christ-centered life sets the foundation on how to properly deal with adversity; money, success, fame, relationships, and any other challenges that life throws at us. This is a very raw and transparent depiction of the challenges birthed by success and how the results of being unprepared for them will affect all your meaningful relationships and your spiritual walk. This book is for anyone who has realized their dream come to fruition, for those who are still crystallizing their own vision and dreams, and for those who want to properly support others in fulfilling their life's aspirations."

"This is a unique book written by a unique person in a unique way. Chris offers lessons learned from personal experiences on the football field and how they relate to life's challenges. His candor is remarkable as he draws from situations faced through accumulative years beginning in middle school, high school, college, and a professional career in football. A must read book."

"Chris was a "Voice of Reason" and had a calming effect on our Defense. You see that in this book *P.R.O.S.* Life is about growth. This book has a way of putting life in its proper perspective. Responsibility is not just an obligation, but also an opportunity. Thank you, Chris, for your insight on parental obligation."

# P.R.O.S.

THE WINNING GAME PLAN FOR
HEALTHY BOUNDARIES BETWEEN
PARENTS AND CHILDREN

# P.R.O.S.

parents relying on †heir seeds

CHRIS HOPE

Published in association with The Fedd Agency, Inc., a literary agency.

Hardback ISBN: 978-1-943217-95-3
Paperback ISBN: 978-1-943217-98-4
eISBN: 978-1-943217-99-1

Printed in the United States of America

First Edition 15 14 13 10 09 / 10 9 8 7 6 5 4 3 2

*To my beautiful, faithful, lovely, and supportive wife Linda
for loving me despite my many flaws and my two adorable
children, Crislyn and Christopher, who are my most prized possessions. To my parents, Randy and Mary Hope, my sister Trebia
Hope, and my brother Rodney Hope. Thank you for all
the experiences, lessons learned, memories, sacrifices, support,
and most importantly, your unconditional love!*

# CONTENTS

# INTRODUCTION

I can barely remember a time when I wasn't on the football field. I was a Pro Bowl defensive back in the NFL and had the honor of being part of the Super Bowl XL Championship team in 2005. Before being drafted into the NFL, I played on a national champion college football team—the 1999 Florida State Seminoles. And before college, I was a high school All-American for the Rock Hill High (South Carolina) Bearcats. And pre-high school, I played on the football team for my middle school and elementary school.

One of the first things I learned as a football player was boundaries. I quickly found out that I had to stay in bounds with the ball if I was going to be able to score. I also learned that being on the field between the white lines was a lot more fun than being on the bench, playing it safe, outside those lines. I worked hard to earn the right to stay on the field wherever I played. I followed and respected the rules of the game. Instead of being restrictive, the boundaries were a comfort to me. Perhaps this is because I knew I belonged within those lines.

My dominance on the field brought me great financial and athletic success. I quickly learned that I needed to put up boundaries in my personal life as well. So, I painted metaphorical white lines in my life, just as there are on a football field, to protect myself, my wife, and my children from those who did not respect the hard work I put in to get where I am today.

I put in years of grinding, grueling hard work to gain recognition in the world of sports. Yet, that was nothing compared to all the hard work I've done to protect myself and my family from those who think they can cross that line and piggyback on my success.

## Unhitch Your Hitch

My experience on and off the field have inspired me to write this book. In addition to putting others on notice, I'm also making myself vulnerable by opening up the doors of my life for you to walk around and see who I am—both my successes and my failures—so you can learn to play within your boundaries and protect those boundaries from those who may only want to take what you have earned.

Imagine, if you will, that you have a trailer hitch hooked up to your life, with the intention of pulling your life's dreams and goals. What happens when someone else hooks their dreams onto your hitch? Chances are, you end up pulling them along and leaving your dreams unfulfilled and maybe theirs, too. What I hope to do in the pages that follow is help you unhitch your hitch from what is not yours to pull. I want to help you become free and establish boundaries so you, too, can achieve your goals and fulfill your dreams.

This is not a book based solely on football. It is a book about living life without regrets. In it, I share some of my story, and since my life has been lived for a great part on a football field, this is where most of my stories take place. So, let's begin. I figured we might as well start with the brightest field and the biggest stage of them all—the Super Bowl.

– CHRIS HOPE

# Chapter 1

# A NOT-SO-SUPER SUNDAY

When 68,000 people gather in a room—even in a very *large* room—the noise is going to be significant. When those people are there to watch an NFL game, the sound is going to be even greater. And when that NFL game is the Super Bowl, well, you can imagine how loud that was. The cheers for my Pittsburgh Steeler teammates and I as we ran onto Ford Field in Detroit that Sunday in February 2006 were louder than the loudest thunderclap you have ever heard. And it was the sweetest sound my ears have ever witnessed.

The Super Bowl. The greatest sporting event on Earth. More than 100 million people around the world would be watching. And there I was, standing on the field along with Ben Roethlisberger, Hines Ward, Troy Polamalu, Joey Porter, and Jerome Bettis—all who are still legends in Pittsburgh to this day. On the other side of the field stood the Seattle Seahawks, featuring that year's MVP, Shaun Alexander. Both teams arrived with winning records, but in just a few short hours, only one would end its season with a win. My teammates and I were determined it would be the men in black and gold claiming that Super Bowl XL trophy.

As we stood on the sidelines listening to Aretha Franklin and Aaron Neville sing the national anthem, my thoughts raced to Rock Hill, South Carolina, where I was a high school All-American my senior year, to Florida State University, where I played in every game as a freshman through to my senior year, to now being the starting free safety for the 2005 AFC Champion, the Pittsburgh Steelers. So many men dream of playing on the biggest stage, yet so few do. It was humbling. I wanted to drink in every moment, every sound, every sight. I locked each into my memory, knowing I might never get to experience it again.

## Kick Off!

My team won the coin flip, and we strategically chose our defense to start the game. I would be on the field right away, which was what I wanted. Both teams traded punts in our first two possessions. On Seattle's third possession, their quarterback, Matt Hasselbeck, lofted a pass to their wide receiver, Darrell Jackson. As Jackson caught the pass, I quickly tackled him, and we both landed violently on the ground. With that hit, all the stress and tension leading up to the Super Bowl vanished. I was playing the game I loved! It was just Darrell, the ball, and me. Football. The green grass within the white lines. No more 68,000 screaming fans. No more TV cameras or sideline reporters. No more agents, contract negotiations, or requests for interviews. And mostly, no more pressure from those I loved (and who loved me) who placed demands on me for tickets or favors before the Big Game, unlike anything I'd ever experienced before. I now had green-and-white borders, and within those borders, I was determined to win.

But the two weeks leading up to the Super Bowl were the most stress-filled weeks I had ever endured. It wasn't football-related pressure. Instead, it was an escalating pressure that comes from the expectations of others! With football, I had prepared for this day since I was a Rock Hill Bearcat. Football was my job, yes, but it was a job I loved and looked forward to every day. As a team, we had prepared for the Super Bowl since July of 2005, working out in the heat at St. Vincent College in Latrobe, Pennsylvania. Every play of every practice, every preseason game, every in-season game, and every playoff game brought us one step closer to our goal: winning the fifth Lombardi Trophy (the award given to the winning team from each Super Bowl) for the great city of Pittsburgh.

## A Long Season

The 2005 season was crazy. We started off red hot, beating Tennessee and Houston before losing a close one to the defending Super Bowl champs, the New England Patriots. Entering the middle part of the season, we were 7-2 and feeling very good about our chances. Then, we lost three games in a row . . . and everyone began to write us off.

I still remember getting beaten on a Sunday night by the Indianapolis Colts, with Peyton Manning as their starting quarterback. They scored on the first play of the game, and it was all downhill from there. After that loss, Coach Bill Cowher came into the locker room and confidently declared to us, "Remember this feeling. We will be back. We'll see the Colts again. Mark my words. Next time, we will be ready!"

It's kind of funny how having a stretch of bad games made it appear to everyone around the league and in the media that the bottom had fallen out. Yet, we were more confident as a team than we were in the previous season, even though our record was worse. I can vividly picture the guys in the locker room saying, "They better not let us into the playoffs. All we gotta do is get in, and it's a wrap!" We knew if we got into the playoffs, we would go all the way this time around. Our confidence was not based on our record that year.

We finished the 2005 regular season 11-5 and had to win our last four games just to make it into the playoffs. We entered the playoffs as the lower-seeded wild card team, and our first opponent in the playoffs was the Bengals, our division rival. I remember my best friend, Lavar, calling me just before that first playoff game. "What are we gonna do this week? I see we got the Bengals at their place," he asked, taunting me in a friendly way.

My response was, "It's over. That's a wrap! We are not worried about the Cincinnati Bengals. Trust me." And we proved that on the field with a 31-17 victory. The week after we beat the Bengals in the wild card game, we traveled back to Indianapolis. Here we were, back on the same field and in the same locker room, just as Coach said we'd be! The Colts were the number one seed and the heavy favorites to win the Super Bowl. Man, were we ready!

I'm happy to report that we handily beat the Colts in their stadium that day. And we followed that up with a win over the Denver Broncos in the AFC Conference Championship Game. After that, we were on our way to the Super Bowl. As the sixth and last seed in the playoffs, the Steelers became the first team in NFL history to win three road games in a row on the way to the Super Bowl. We were true "road warriors."

It was demanding work, for sure, but that was not the only mounting pressure I was feeling. A pressure most people don't realize happens leading up to the Big Game. Although I was wired for football and the hard work that makes a champion in that sport, the overwhelming stress stemmed from the enormous expectations outside the world of football that others placed on me.

## Trouble in Paradise

It started the night we defeated the Denver Broncos in the AFC Championship Game at Mile High Stadium. After a humble and small celebration in the locker room with my teammates, our coaches, and the people from our personnel department who traveled with us to the game, we loaded onto our team buses and headed straight to the airport. My phone was flooded with calls, text messages, and voicemails—many from people I hadn't spoken to in years, and some I didn't recognize or know how they had even gotten my phone number.

Now, I want to be clear as I say this. I have a wonderful family and a great support team of friends who have helped me get to where I am today. The Hope family is very close. In fact, as a kid, my big brother, Rodney, and I watched football every Sunday after church, sharing a blanket on the living room floor of our little house. Over many years of watching so many games together, we developed a sibling tradition on Super Bowl Sunday. Unlike many kids who play sports today, we did not only play and like all sports, we were fans and somewhat historians of the sports we played. I'm a firm believer that in any and everything you do in life, you have to know and understand your history. Because to know where you're going, you need to know where you came from. Super Bowl Sunday was exactly that for my brother and me. Every time it rolled around, it was like a college refresher course or a history lesson on America's most beloved game on its biggest stage.

Each year before the Big Game, we would watch and relive all the highlights from all the previous Super Bowls shown by the network leading up to kickoff. Our faces were practically glued to the tube of the TV screen. I can still hear my dad yelling, "Rodney, get back off the TV like that. You're going to be blind as a bat!" (Go figure, I was the one who ended up having to wear glasses.) We would've settled for the experience of just being *at* the game, let alone playing in it. To dream of playing in a game with such magnitude was too big for even Walt Disney to dream. However, it still didn't stop us from wanting to climb through the TV and be in the Super Bowl—to smell the air, hear the crowd, and touch the field.

Fast forward several years and here I was, standing on Ford Field in Detroit, trying to take it all in. In a word, it was incredible.

My football career was not just about me, though. It never has been. It was just as important for my family and close friends to come along and experience this magic carpet ride as it was for me to continue to provide them with the memories. But never in a million years did it ever cross my mind that the biggest game in all of sports would be the game that divided my family. When I say divide my family, I mean my dad and mom literally expected me to split the number of tickets I was allotted to buy right down the middle: half to his side of the family and the other half to her side of the family. My parents must have forgotten there were four of us just in our immediate household, not including me. How crazy was that?

Most importantly, what about who *I* wanted to invite or who *I* thought deserved to be at the game? My girlfriend, my grandparents, my cousin Gerald Dixon—who took me in when times were tough in the Hope house—my best friend, or any of the amazing and influential coaches or teachers who helped me become the player and man I am today.

It was my game, right? I busted my behind and put in all the work to get there, right? I wanted to say to them: *Remember all those days running in the hot sun? I know you don't, because I was out there by myself.*

On one of the biggest stages in the world in which the Hope name and family would be recognized and receive national exposure, it hurts my heart to say that behind closed doors we were fussing and fighting like immature children because of assumptions, entitlement, expectancy, greed, hate, jealousy, and selfishness. All these emotions were exposed and brought to the forefront. These feelings were all threatening to overwhelm the immense joy that comes with reaching your life goal. Shouldn't family add to your joy, not subtract from it?

I felt as though my parents were asking me to pick a side. It was almost like they were competing to see whose side of the family would be represented the most. It was so bad and ugly, I left home and headed back to Pittsburgh with the intention of not letting anyone attend the game.

I think I fell out with just about everyone that week, all within a few days before the Super Bowl. My girlfriend, whom I eventually married, wanted her dad to attend the game. My brother wanted his girlfriend, whom he eventually married, to attend the game. And I felt like my parents were each promising tickets to family members and friends who had helped them out in the past. These pressures pained and stressed me for days. Not to mention the anxiety of organizing hotel rooms, plane tickets, and travel arrangements for my family and friends— whom I knew for sure were coming to the game—prior to the week of practice before we even headed to Detroit. By the time it was all said and done, I was worried I would be playing in the game for free by spending all the money I would earn for playing the game on plane tickets, game tickets, hotel rooms, and food for family and friends.

The stress and pressure began to wear me down and started to become a major distraction. Something had to be done and time was running out. I had to hurt some feelings and make some tough decisions on who I wanted to attend the game.

If you ask anyone who really knows me, I hate being the bearer of bad news or being responsible for hurting someone else's feelings. But the part that hurt the most was when my brother, whom I grew up watching this very game with for years, decided to opt out and give his game ticket to his girlfriend. That hurt stuck with me for years. I guess at the time, he thought just like everyone else, that this wouldn't be my first and last trip to the Super Bowl. I wasn't mad at his girlfriend for accepting the ticket. Well, that's not entirely true. To be honest, I felt like she should've denied the ticket and said, "There's no way I'm going to your brother's Super Bowl game while you watch it on TV in some bar or hotel room."

Yet, even in this stressful situation, some good did shine through the clouds. I realized I have one of the most unselfish and giving men in the world as a brother. As I mentioned earlier, my brother and his girlfriend ended up getting married and blessing our family with a beautiful baby girl, who just happened to be born on my birthday. Now, that's what you call making up for your mistake and coming through big in the clutch! I guess I can forgive them now. Although, the sad part is, I was never fortunate enough to make it back to the Super Bowl. I came really close two more times, but my teammates and I couldn't get over the hump.

As for the rest of my family and friends, I rented out a restaurant in my hometown that had several large-screen TVs, pool tables, video games, drinks, and food. I paid for everything and allowed them to party, relax, and watch the game. It was a huge success! Both sides of my family, including my grandparents, came out and had a blast. My uncle recorded the entire night's festivities and mailed me the DVD. And what I witnessed on that DVD made me realize that good did come from all the craziness that led up to the game.

A big part of preparing for an upcoming football game is watching footage of the previous game, learning from mistakes, and improving your techniques. When I watched the footage of my family at that restaurant, seeing both sides of my family breaking bread together, witnessing all the love, happiness, excitement, and oneness that was evident that night, it made everything worthwhile. That family celebration has to be one of the greatest feelings and memories I have of the Super Bowl. I truly believe there is some good in every situation we are faced with, but we must be patient and willing to find it.

We won Super Bowl XL, defeating the Seahawks 21-10. That victory will live with me forever. Yet, I know there are greater victories to be gained in life than what I earned that night in 2006. I'm still searching and looking for answers, carefully maneuvering through the hard parts of loving relationships, looking for the authentic substance. I won't stop. In fact, my last name won't allow me to. Plus, I have even bigger goals to achieve.

In the pages ahead, I want to share with you the important lessons I have learned through my experiences over the years, both good and bad, that may help you in navigating the rough seas of your relationships. Our goal must be one and the same: to make every day a Super Bowl victory in all that we do.

# Chapter 2

# A GAME OF INCHES

A few months ago, while writing this book, I went home to celebrate my mom's 60th birthday. A lot of our family, and many of her closest friends, were there to join in on the celebration. To be completely transparent, I was hesitant at first to invest all that money into a birthday party, because I wondered if it was worth the expense. To be fair, it was a very nice party. My wife, Linda, helped me realize that no amount of money would compare to how happy, excited, appreciated, loved, and supported my mom would feel from us having this party for her. The joy my mom felt that night will be something I'll never forget. The party was all about her. And she owned that night.

Then, right during the chaos, food, laughter, and dancing, I realized something was missing. Many other important people from our family—either because they were deceased or they had chosen not to come—weren't there. Their absence was a painful reminder to me. It reminded me that no matter how good things are, or how many obstacles we overcome as a family, there will still be bittersweet moments. This celebration was one of those times.

To be a professional athlete was one part of my dream when I was growing up. However, most kids don't dream of throwing sixtieth birthday parties for their parents. That's because in dreams no one ever gets old. And when deciding to do something for your parents, there are never any regrets. Especially not any painful ones. Contrary to what many may believe, there were several painful moments in the Hope house growing up. As teenagers, my brother, sister, and I sometimes felt like we were growing up in a "house of potential." It's what some people refer to as being in the "rat race." Unfortunately, potential can work both ways: You have the potential to be good or the potential to be bad. And it means absolutely nothing until you choose how you're going to use it.

Living on Saluda Street in Rock Hill, South Carolina, we were always struggling, fussing, fighting, and usually splitting one piece of steak five different ways, with the steak having more fat than meat on it. For that very reason, I still don't get overly excited about a big, juicy steak. On a positive note, I'm also not a fan of red meat, so maybe I'll live longer.

There was only one bathroom in our house, and all five of us had to share it. Often, one of us would shower while someone else would use the toilet or be in front of the mirror trying to get dressed for the day, fighting through all the steam that covered the mirror.

The statement of "less is more" didn't make sense to me until I had the opportunity to experience more. Growing up, we had less of everything, but we had the idea of family—the "Hope" of family. At least we were all together in the same crab bucket, so to speak. We all had the same fight, same hustle, same last name, so it appeared we were all pulling in the same direction. But I wanted more for us. Even as a child, I wanted a family that would be more than just a collection of people with the same last name living in the same house.

Today, we all have more stuff—bigger and better possessions. But we don't have each other—at least not in the same way it felt to me as a kid. Jesus said in Matthew 16:26, "For what profit is it to a man if he gains the whole world, and loses his own soul?" Like Jesus said, the pleasures of life can't fulfill us, so we might as well focus on what matters most.

As I've grown through the years, with much help and wisdom from my wife, I've learned a lot about family and what healthy relationships look like. I'm also learning about real and meaningful success. We have all been blessed with the potential and talents to possibly stumble across success at some point in our lives. I mean, even a garbage can is blessed with a steak from time to time. Yet, it isn't until success turns into significance that we can truly say we are winning in life.

There's an old saying in football that illustrates how close the gap is between winning and losing. "It's a game of inches, men, and everyone is in pursuit of those same inches. It's our job to go out and fight to find them." My high school coach would say this to us. This phrase must've been taught in some secret coaches' academy, because I've had it quoted to me on every team I've been a part of. But it's not only true in football, it's also true in life.

At some point, all of us will be faced with adversity. It's how we choose to respond to the adversity that makes us different. Adversity doesn't just build character; it helps reveal character. As the old proverb goes, "The same boiling water that softens potatoes hardens eggs." In other words, significance comes from what you make of your circumstances. We all strive for success and try to avoid failure. Yet, sometimes success creates adversity—with friends and family—and even within ourselves.

It's not always the fame that gets to successful people first. It starts with the walls that successful people must build once they enter a different economic threshold. As a result, their personal lives and relationships will begin to be challenged, which, in turn, causes them to protect themselves. Their time, talents, and gifts begin to suffer, because they are more focused on creating and enforcing boundaries instead of working on their craft. The same walls they build to protect themselves eventually become the same walls that imprison them. Comedian Dave Chappelle says that "success causes a person's humanity to diminish, and then they become something else to people."

The difference between successful and unsuccessful people is that successful people are willing to do what the unsuccessful ones will not. Successful people don't have quitting in their blood. They don't quit after a victory or a defeat. They press on, trying to find a way to get better. On your journey to success, if you can recognize and truly believe this in your heart, you will stop less and go farther. No matter how bad the situation is, there is always some good in it. But we must be willing to roll up our sleeves and dig through the mess and pain to find it.

I wrote this book after grappling with feelings of guilt, frustration, and pain. I was desperate for answers, and I'm a firm believer in what Coach Paul, also known as Paul the Apostle, said in Romans 8:28: "And we know that all things work together for good to those who love God, to those who are called according to His purpose." The moment I turned it all over to God, I knew I needed to write this book—for myself and my family, but most importantly, for all of you.

## We Are All Children

When I was a little boy, my Grandma Christine used to say to me as we'd alternate combing each other's hair, "Once a man and twice a child! You're getting older, and I'm getting younger. One day you're gonna have to take care of and look after me." I remember sitting there being perplexed by her statement. It wasn't until I was twenty-four years of age, back home in South

Carolina after winning Super Bowl XL, that I understood what my grandmother was saying to me. My regular daily routine, when I was back in my hometown, consisted of stopping by my grandmother's house to spend time with her after my early morning workout. As she laid her frail frame and unstable head on my lap, I fed her a fruit cup and began to comb her hair. That's when it hit me. I fully understood the wisdom she shared with me so many years ago when she said, "Chris, one day you're gonna have to take care of me." My eyes tear up every time I think about that day with my grandmother, because her prophecy came true right before my eyes.

We all will have two brief, still moments in our lives: when we are born and when we die. We all use the expression, "Life is too short," but do we truly understand how short life is? I will sum it up for you. Life is as short as the dash between the birth date and death date displayed on your tombstone.

## Bringing Success Home

All of us want to know that our family will be there for us. But family relationships can be pretty complicated, right? It's almost inevitable that during some season of one's life, the parent will rely on their son or daughter to be there for them in some capacity. The question is: When does this transition take place? Is there an age requirement for this transaction? I only ask because depending on the situation, some parents these days declare for early retirement, expecting their kids to provide and care for them, whether the kids are emotionally, financially, physically, or spiritually prepared to do so. What are the right expectations for the parent and the child? How do we expect less from one another but gain more from each other? When does the honor or privilege of having the ability to take care of your parents turn into a burden or an unmerited responsibility?

In Exodus 20:12, the Bible instructs us to "Honor your father and your mother, that your days may be long upon the land which the Lord your God is giving you." I have to wonder, what's the correct definition of honoring? Does honoring come with a price tag, credit card, diploma, bank account, or a new house and car? It seems that it's left up to us to figure out, in specific detail, daily, what honoring our parents truly means.

As a kid, I always dreamed of becoming a famous athlete, actor, pilot, engineer, architect, or business owner. I sincerely believed with all my heart that one day I'd reach the pinnacle in whatever profession I chose. But year after year, sports continued to choose me. Growing up in church, I often heard the old Yiddish proverb, "Man makes a plan, and God laughs." I knew one day, I'd experience success, but I honestly didn't know how God would allow it to manifest in my life.

In my quest for success, there was a simple, constant motivation: I wanted to make my parents proud. But what kid doesn't? The American Dream always was, and still is, to have a loving spouse, healthy kids, a dog, and a beautiful house with a white picket fence around it. For an athlete, the American Dream is slightly different. It is to become a professional in a sport, sign a big contract, and then buy your parents their dream home with a white picket fence around it. Most sports movies or television shows depicting a kid being drafted into the professional ranks portrays this same notion. This idea has brainwashed the athletic world and, to some extent, the entertainment and entrepreneurial world. More specifically, these expectations affected my thinking into believing when I did make it, I owed it all to my parents, siblings, distant cousins, friends, coaches, communities, schools, and churches.

And those expectations appear on both sides of the table.

## Success and Uncertainty

Successful athletes, artists, architects, doctors, lawyers, preachers, surgeons, and businesspeople don't know how to respond to this sense of family entitlement, because it's all new to them. Regardless of that fact, the way they respond will be very critical. Their initial response will set the tone for many battles down the road. I don't know where you're from or what area code you live in, but where I'm from the motto is, "When one of us makes it out, we all make it out."

What athlete, or successful person for that matter, would knowingly make a commitment to take care of a group of adults for the rest of their lives, when the contract the athlete signs with his or her respected team isn't a lifetime, guaranteed deal? Most people, including many professional athletes, don't realize how fragile their bodies really are—or how breakable their employment contracts are. A long career isn't promised to anyone, no matter the profession. Success is to be enjoyed and is certainly to be shared. But success, and the pressure that it brings, also reveals cracks in our character and exposes flaws in what were thought to be solid relationships.

As future professional athletes, actors, actresses, coaches, CEOs, entertainers, entrepreneurs, dentists, doctors, lawyers, writers, or any other influential person, how we prepare for our success is key to being able to enjoy our success. For example, drivers don't apply for car insurance after they have an accident. They already have car insurance in place, so they're prepared for an accident. And, just like drivers, the time to prepare to handle success is now. As parents, we must prepare our children for real success and then expect it to happen. As a result, we won't be surprised by our children's success but very much prepared for it. Then all that's left to do is guard our hearts against wrong attitudes or selfish ambitions.

My hope in sharing my learned lessons and life experiences with you is to help you step into the best and most productive version of yourself. My goal is also to make sure when you finally arrive at your purpose in life, you're still associated with everyone you started life with. I say this because life is about turning the things you really want to do into things you have already done.

In the words of the Grammy Award-winning and multiplatinum recording artist Drake, "Money is supposed to make a difference but not make us different." I share this, because I want you to not only reach your own individual goals and dreams but also to enjoy the success with your loved ones and to help others along the way. These lessons will help you to maintain success and continue to grow personally, spiritually, and financially.

Most of all, I hope you can learn from my struggles, stay inbounds with your friends and family, and celebrate life to the fullest every day. Always remember: We come into this world looking like our parents, but we leave this world looking like our decisions.

## TURNOVERS

- Don't sacrifice long-term significance for short-term success. What might seem like a path to success could steer you away from significance.
- Don't neglect today's duties for "potential." Often, "potential" becomes a trap for laziness or self-indulgence.
- Avoiding struggles and adversity can keep you from success and significance. Play to win rather than playing to not lose. There is a big difference.
- Be aware that many others will want to hitch a ride on your gravy train.

## TAKEAWAYS

- It's right and proper to give honor to those whom honor is due, such as your parents and grandparents. It is also right and proper to keep that honor from growing into unhealthy expectations. Find the right ways to give honor while keeping your boundaries.
- Prepare for success now, even if you don't see it just yet. When you have reached a level of success, it will be too late to prepare for how to handle it.
- What makes a family is not what they possess, but what possesses them.
- You can't control your circumstances, but you can control how you respond to your circumstances.

# Chapter 3

# LEGACY VERSUS EXPECTATION

When I think about my great-grandfather, a familiar and often-used saying from Proverbs 13:22 comes to mind: "A good man leaves an inheritance to his children's children . . ." Even though I never met the man, his legacy met my life and has continued to have an impact on my family, which will have a ripple effect for generations to come. When I was drafted into the NFL, the first thing on my to-do list—after continuous days of praise and thanks to God—was to build my parents their dream home. This is a similar dream for many other athletes in the sports world. Notice I used the word "home" instead of the word "house." I did that because there's a big difference between the two. I was raised in a house on Saluda Street, but I never experienced living in a home as a child. The way I differentiate between the two is summed up in the saying, "A house is made by hands, but a home is made by hearts."

Home is not just a place; it's also a feeling. For instance, anyone can stumble across some good sleep in a house if the body is tired enough, but it's challenging for an individual to find complete rest and peace while sleeping anywhere other than in their own home. That is, if they are truly being honest and are bold enough to call where they grew up, or the place they are currently living, a home. When you add love to the atmosphere in a house, it magically turns into a home. Which brings complete understanding and validation to the famous saying, "There's no place like home."

I assume every kid shares this same dream, or at least it's one of their biggest goals, to one day be blessed enough to show their parents how much they appreciate them—either by monetary assistance, gifts, their spiritual walk, or heavy doses of gratitude. Personally, I can't express the joy or put into words how I felt by being able to accomplish all of this, while seeing my own dreams become a reality.

As I began my quest to build my parents their dream home, finding a great neighborhood or the perfect location was the easiest part of the entire process. My parents inherited an acre of land that was passed down from my great-grandparents to my grandparents and then to my parents. With the hardest part out of the way, I was super excited and could not wait to get the project started. This would be the biggest and best surprise my parents had ever received. Little did I know, I was about to get a shocking surprise as well.

# Reparations

As I started to do the groundwork to see how much it was going to take to make one of my biggest dreams become a reality, I was informed that the property had a lien on it. What? A lien? I learned that a lien means that another party has a financial claim to the land, and the debt must be paid in full before the property can be discharged, sold, or, in my case, developed. I remember asking the gentleman at the records department, "What do you mean this property has a lien on it? Are you referring to a lean as in, a slope in the property, which is the very reason we call it "The Hill"? Are you sure you are looking at the right name and address?"

His reply crushed me. "I'm absolutely positive, Mr. Hope." I went from being shocked to embarrassed to angry to hurt to disappointed. It was like I was being reminded that no matter how far we had come as a family, we couldn't escape our past. To think of all the sacrifices, blood loss, shedding of tears, and all the countless hours of hard work just to obtain the land makes my blood boil to this day. I mean the land was gifted, free of charge, to my parents from my grandparents. But many years earlier, the land had been used as collateral for credit toward something that I'm sure benefited our family at the time. But in that moment, when speaking to the gentleman in the records department, it was excruciating to hear that my parents did not outright own the land they were gifted, and it was probably the only item they had ever owned in their lives at that point. The sad part is, they didn't even have to work for the land, and it didn't cost them a dime.

It is disheartening to know that we can sacrifice and build a legacy of wealth, land, businesses, and other valuable assets for our children, and future generations to come, only to relinquish all our control and not know if they will be good stewards. At the end of the day, all we can do is educate them while we are here and pray that they do right by our beliefs when we are gone.

King Solomon expressed this to us in Ecclesiastes 2:18-19: "Then I hated all my labor in which I had toiled under the sun, because I must leave it to the man who will come after me. And who knows whether he will be wise or a fool? Yet he will rule over all my labor." In short, I learned that the financial damage had to be repaired before the future dream home could be built. This scenario sounds about right, or at least very familiar to me growing up. Two steps forward, four steps backward. Instead of building onto a legacy, I was making reparations for past mistakes, financial hardships, and unwise choices. Instead of creating an inheritance for my children's children and the next generations, I was paying off debt and being held back by decisions made by previous generations.

It reminds me of one of the worst setbacks in the game of football: committing a pre-snap penalty. It's like a self-inflicted wound that impedes the progress and stops the momentum of the offense. You are literally causing yourself and your team to go the wrong way! Pre-snap penalties almost always result in a change of possession. Most times, penalties are just too hard to overcome. Nothing gets under a head coach's skin more than a pre-snap penalty. This is because it can be very detrimental to the outcome of a game.

Just like a coach after a pre-snap foul, I was upset. In my case, it was about the financial implications of the lien. I just kept thinking about how we could have used that money toward another phase of the project or to bless someone else in need. But on a deeper level, I was upset that my family had veered from God's design for a legacy of abundance. It was like my parents came to a fork in the road and decided to go straight. The Bible teaches that a good man is supposed to leave an inheritance to his kids' kids, not to his parents, siblings, uncles, aunts, cousins, friends, and communities. In other words, everyone should try to have an impact and influence, not just on his or her own family, but also on the next generation by paying it forward.

My great-grandfather, Henry "Boss" Wylie, gave me a living illustration of what King Solomon meant when he wrote Proverbs 13:22. My great-grandfather was the trailblazer responsible for igniting this legacy for our family by leaving each one of his kids an acre of land to be maintained, kept in the family, and passed down to the next generation: a reciprocation of his blessing. Even though it was unfortunate and disappointing that I had to pay off the lien to get our property back in our sole possession, I am grateful to say that a few years later, my parents had their dream home built on the land my grandparents blessed them with. Ironically, their home sits on the front of a major highway, back in my hometown, where people constantly drive back and forth, in awe and amazement. Apparently, God turned my family's mess into a message.

## Expectation Versus Legacy

In this next section, we're going to see how expectations look backward and legacy looks forward. Expectations are the debts I am paying for that had nothing to do with me; whereas, legacies are the benefits that future generations will reap because of the hard work and discipline of others. The great investor Warren Buffet says, "Someone is sitting in the shade today because someone planted a tree a long time ago."

Can you see how different the two cycles are?

As an athlete, I was always taught that you are either getting better or getting worse. No one ever stays the same. This is because we are always evolving and striving to become better versions of ourselves. My definition of change is not allowing or letting the way we've grown accustomed to doing things in the past prevent us from being open to the new opportunities God is presenting to us today. In fact, the most constant thing in life is change itself. We should all embrace change, because it's inevitable. Don't be like concrete, all mixed up in your feelings and forever stuck in your ways.

Since becoming a father, my life's biggest goal is to follow in the footsteps of my great-grandfather and leave an inheritance to my children's children. But how are we supposed to plan for tomorrow, when those around us only think about, and live for, today? I'm expected to pay it forward to the next generation, not continue to give it back to the generations before me.

Legacy is a blessing. Honoring your parents is a blessing. Expectation, however, is a burden. The experience of building my parent's home opened my eyes to the vast difference between legacy and expectation. Don't get me wrong, I love and want to be generous, but when generosity is expected, it becomes a debt that will cause even a billionaire to grow alligator arms when the check comes. Seeds of expectation harvest crops of debt and disappointment. And the Bible is clear that debt is bad in finances and relationships. Proverbs 22:7 states, "The rich rule over the poor, and the borrower is servant to the lender." And in Psalm 37:21, we are told, "The wicked borrow and do not repay, but the righteous show mercy and give."

My wife and I also desire a legacy of mercy and generosity. After all, we know how highly-favored and blessed we are. We have received so much mercy, grace, and forgiveness throughout our lives that it would be disgraceful if we didn't share our blessings with others. I am not against people helping their parents and family. I take great pride in having the ability to assist my family when needed, and I've gladly made it my responsibility to do so. The point is to aim higher, toward future generations. This is the only way we will break the cycle of debt and dysfunction and begin to live our lives the way God intended. We must make a choice to live for our legacy and not for ourselves, whether we have been on the receiving end of financial blessings or on the giving end.

In other words, honoring our mothers, fathers, sisters, brothers, extended family, and friends means having clear boundaries and a clear vision of what the future looks like. Honoring our parents and those we love doesn't come with a checkbook, a credit card, or a bank account.

## Givers and Takers

Singer and songwriter Rachel Wolchin says, "Givers need to set limits because takers rarely do." Despite the temptation to "help out," we must realize that dependency ultimately hurts people and destroys relationships. Relationships must be bilateral. They can't just be all withdrawals and no deposits. The tipping point is when "help" becomes expected. An old man once told me that when you give someone something for the first time, they politely say thank you, and they are truly grateful and appreciative. The next time you offer something to that same person, they politely decline and hand over to you their wish list. As a parent, when you start relying on your kids to make a way for you, you have crossed into the "red zone." As a giver, when you start to stunt the growth of the people around you, you have crossed over into the red zone. Red is the color of fire and blood and is often associated with words like "passion," "energy," "emotion," "desire," "danger," and "war." In my profession, being in the red zone is only good for the team who has the ball, or, to my point on this matter, the power.

Givers, you must be responsible in how you give. This means honestly counting the full cost of the blessings and gifts you give to your loved ones and not making financial decisions based on emotion—especially unhealthy emotions like guilt. Yes, you may want your mom to have a nice car, but have you counted the cost, the taxes, the maintenance, the gas, the car washes, and the insurance? You should ask yourself, are you going to be responsible for and okay with all the never-ending expenses as well?

Clear communication builds relationships. Unspoken assumptions undermine relationships. Parents must not set their child up for failure by accepting a gift without first counting the cost. If you receive a gift and you know you can't afford to maintain it, be a mature adult and say to your son or daughter that you don't know if you can be responsible for the related expenses. Be the same person your child has always looked up to and respected from the time they learned to talk and walk and say you don't know if you can meet the expectations that he or she has concerning the gift.

Let's face it: The Bible nails it when we read in Timothy 6:10, "For the love of money is the root of all evil." Money can be like a drug. Just like there are two sides to every story, in every relationship and situation there are also two sides. In the issue of substance abuse, we have the user and the dealer. One does not exist without the other. When it comes to money and material things, don't love either. Instead, ask yourself if your actions are building a legacy or paying reparations. With reparations, there is an attempt to fix something from the past to pacify or overcompensate for someone's lack of resources, support, or opportunities. It's almost like you are trying to bring that person back up to speed or place them on a level playing field. Sometimes, this is the right thing to do, and it can come from a good place. But to remain in that mode, and feed unhealthy expectations, is to rob future generations of their legacy and to handicap the very person you are attempting to help.

Sometimes, when we do things for people, we are short-circuiting what they need to discover on their own to fulfill their true potential. Bishop Joseph Warren Walker, III, pastor of Mt. Zion Baptist Church of Nashville, Tennessee, and presiding bishop of the Full Gospel Baptist Church Fellowship International, often tells people who are going through trying times that God has them exactly where He wants them to be. He also shares that God will never deliver us from what He's trying to develop in us. That's because He doesn't need our ability; He just needs our availability. He wants our obedience. God doesn't need help from you, me, or anyone else to pull a person through a situation. As stated in 2 Corinthians 12:9, He might not always deliver us out of every bad situation we are in, but He will give us the grace to sustain our minds until we get through it.

A caterpillar doesn't become a beautiful butterfly until all the stages of metamorphosis are complete. It is the process of fighting to get out of the cocoon that allows the wings that will bear the butterfly into the air to develop. You should leave the cocoon alone, or you will mess up or interrupt the process. When we get ahead of God, we may end up blessed for a moment, but we end up unhappy and unfulfilled in the long run. And boy have I learned that the hard way.

To be honest, I enjoyed stepping up and getting it done— on the football field and in my extended family. I always made sure I took care of my responsibilities and made my plays first. Then, I tried to cover up for my teammates when they didn't make their plays, even when I shouldn't have. In those instances, if I was wrong, the whole team lost out. When I started playing God by trying to make up for other people's losses, misfortunes, hopes, and dreams, I dishonored God.

## Choices

As you experience success at any level, you must make a clear and intentional decision for legacy, not reparations. I know, it sounds tough and might even seem cold. But we only get one life to live, and you are only responsible for your life. Parents, your kids can't live for you, and you can't live through your children. That's not what you really want, anyway, is it?

The spirit of expectation is based on entitlement, greed, and selfishness. Expectations grow like weeds, and they are never satisfied until they take over everything. It's like buying someone breakfast, only to see them get upset when you don't buy them lunch. We all carry unspoken expectations for each other, especially for those we are closest to. However, the only expectations you should live up to are the ones you place on yourself. I believe having expectations for yourself is a natural part of life. It's when we force our expectations on others and then react negatively toward them when they don't respond how we had hoped that we get into trouble.

Consequently, we all need to learn how to relinquish our attachments to the results of our expectations. We all will struggle with this at some point in our lives. And when it happens, that's when it's time to call a time-out and look in the mirror. If you don't and you begin to feed the "entitlement monster," it will continue to grow. And, one day, it will consume you and all your meaningful relationships.

When I was dating, my (now) wife, Linda, I would often buy her lavish gifts and have big surprises for her on her birthday to express my love for her. After a few years of spoiling her, I thought to myself, *If I keep buying bigger and better gifts, I'm going to run out of surprises for her once we get married, or I'll go broke trying to top last year's gift!"* And Linda loved and appreciated the gifts, but she treasured our relationship above all and never expected or pressured me into doing anything out of the ordinary for her.

There's a quote that says, "Give a person an inch, and they'll want a foot. Give them a foot, they'll want a yard. Give them a yard, and they'll want a swimming pool." There is responsibility and blame on both sides when you operate in this manner. It becomes very hard to say no to the people you love. When you do, it makes you feel guilty, selfish, unaccountable, or like you turned your back on them. Then pride kicks in. From an athlete's perspective, or from someone who is used to being the provider, having to say, "I can't do that" is very difficult. In fact, I don't think many successful people, at least those in my profession, even know the word "can't." When someone tells us we can't do something, we try our hardest to prove them wrong. Most athletes are firm believers in Philippians 4:13, which states, "I can do all things through Christ Jesus who strengthens me." Furthermore, people with money don't ever want others to think they are not doing as well financially as they once were. But it's all pride. As givers, we should do what the late Michael Jackson said and start with the man in the mirror.

Many years ago, before my NFL career, my uncle paid an expensive bill for my mom. He paid it generously, without fanfare, and with no expectations. But for some reason, I felt obligated to pay him back. And I did. But why did I feel so obligated? That's my question for you.

Legacy or expectation—the choice is a matter of motivation. If you are on the giving end of the equation, are you giving out of a false sense of expectation or guilt? Do you feel like you owe someone for your success or blessings? If you are on the receiving end, have you become dependent on your children or family members? Do you live by the unwritten proverb that proclaims, "That's just what families do. We pitch in and help each other out."? In either situation, it's time to get real and communicate the truth to one another.

## Dreams for Our Legacy

Every parent's dream is to provide a life for their children that's better than the life they had when they were growing up. That same belief isn't any different in the Hope house. My wife and I are trying to leave an inheritance—something for our kids to stand on and pass on—which includes finances. But really it's about so much more. The most important part of our legacy will come twenty years from now, when our children are living well and honorably, positively affecting the world in some way or another. That will be the most important part of our legacy. Adding value to their last name and being a child of God is what's most important to me. A parent's job is to encourage their kids to develop a joy for life and a great urge to follow their dreams. The best way to do this isn't by pressuring them into doing something we would like to see them do. Instead, it's to expose them to options and to help them develop a personal set of tools to become whatever they want to become in life.

The thought of legacy makes me eager to wake up the minute my head hits the pillow at night. I've always strived to be a person who wakes up every morning without an alarm clock due to my zeal and zest for life. I refuse to call it dreaming. Instead, I refer to it as "nighttime daydreaming," because I am rarely completely sound asleep. I'm not anxious. Instead, I'm super excited and eager to see all my dreams come to fruition. The little mouse in my brain often pulls its tiny hamstrings, trying to run as fast as it can to keep pace with my thinking. I'm always chasing after greatness and preparing to transition from successful to significant. That's what life is about to me.

We all need to take the advice of flight attendants: "Put on your oxygen mask before assisting others." We sometimes become so overwhelmed—physically and emotionally run down—trying to help others that we forget to take care of ourselves. If we can't give ourselves our best, we definitely won't be able to or be motivated to give our best to others. There's nothing selfish about giving yourself permission to recharge your battery and to plan winning strategies. We're all either preparing to succeed or preparing to fail. As Benjamin Franklin said, "By failing to prepare, you are preparing to fail."

To prevent being blindsided by other people's expectations, or consumed by someone else's assumptions, make plans for *your* future, and include those you care about the most, then carry out your plans. I refuse to die with my seed in my pocket and leave my job for someone else to do. But I have one big dilemma: How can I pay it forward if I always have to reach back-ward? The answer can be hard to accept. We can't live for the future and the past. We must choose. We must also embrace the paradox and stop dying while we are still living and start living like we are dying.

Just remember: Living a full life isn't about how long you live. It's about living out your purpose while you're still living and then doing something so remarkable and rare that it out-lives you.

## TURNOVERS

- Don't give irresponsibly, by showering your loved ones with gifts, without first counting the cost.
- Don't make the mistake of becoming an enabler or allowing your child to enable you.
- Be careful about getting ahead of God's plans for you and your loved ones, which can cause you to do things out of guilt.
- Don't force your expectations on your loved ones.

## TAKEAWAYS

- Think about the end in the beginning. All good things come to an end, so be prepared.
- Pay off debts and clean up your loved ones' credit instead of showering them with gifts, such as houses, cars, jewelry, and exotic trips.
- Prepare for your transition from being successful to becoming significant. Stop trying to always fit in. Instead, become comfortable standing out.
- Invest in your family's future and don't blow all your resources on your family's past. You can't pay it forward to future generations if you're always reaching back to help the generations from the past.

# Chapter 4

# PAIN VERSUS GLORY

Professional athletes are best friends with pain. On the football field, we receive pain, and we dish it out. Believe it or not, many of my most painful moments in life never happened to me on the football field. I would love to say it's because I always delivered the pain to the opposing team, but the real pain I've experienced is actually directly related to the many heartbreaking and traumatic experiences off the field. While playing football, I experienced one of the greatest paradoxes of my life. For my entire career, I trained my body to inflict and absorb pain on the field, but I quickly realized how unprepared I was for the bumps and bruises life would hand out off the field. And boy, did it hit me like a ton of bricks.

Most people only see the good side of life experienced by those in the NFL, in any other elite sport, or in any professional career, while observing from their "nosebleed seats." They see the lifestyle, the money, the cars, the clothes, the houses, the exotic trips, the notoriety—basically, people taking pictures and wanting autographs—but what they don't see is all the pain and responsibility that come with success.

For me, one of the most painful experiences was learning to say one little word. And I believe saying this word is crucial for each one of us if we are ever fortunate enough to experience real success and find true peace and happiness in the process. Before I share this important word with you, I want to share a bit more about myself.

## Eyes on the Prize

I've never had a drink of alcohol or smoked a cigarette in my life. I've also never sold drugs or taken anything that wasn't mine, and I've never been violent—off the field, at least. With that said, I am far from being God's number-one, overall draft choice when it comes to selecting his most obedient follower. But when it comes to something I want in my life, I won't allow anything to stop me or get in my way of achieving it.

I'm sharing this with you, because when it comes to chasing success, you must be disciplined, determined, and focused on what you're chasing. A wise man once shared with me, "Chasing after one rabbit will be difficult enough, so chasing after two will be close to impossible. Unless, you are only chasing them for the exercise with no real intention of ever catching them." It takes a different kind of discipline to be great. Whether in high school, college, or as a professional, I've always had the ability to lock in and block out everything else going on around me. Very similar to thoroughbreds when racing, I learned how to put on the blinders and live by one of my favorite mottos, "Keep the main thang the main thang." The sacrifices I've been willing to make over the years have never been greater than the rewards I've pursued. With that said, I want you to know that you must love the process just as much as you love the prize. When everyone else was going to parties and hanging out, I was working out and studying. The night before games, some of my teammates would stay up late watching movies or even chose to push the team curfew to the limit by partying; whereas, I chose to get a good night's rest.

I did this, because I knew I had to be at my best to fulfill my dreams. Although I was a great athlete, football was, and always has been, my Plan B. Having said that, and in the interest of being completely transparent, anything other than becoming a professional athlete would've been a disappointment for me. So, I challenged myself and conditioned my mind into thinking the NFL was my only way up and out. I made myself believe I had no other options by repeating one little word.

## Learn This Word

To be great, you must be willing to sacrifice. Which brings us back to that important little word and the difference between success and failure. The difference between being good or just being good enough. The difference between being mediocre in everything and excellent at nothing. This word has the power to determine your destiny, and, depending on how and when you use it, it will affect your entire future. This word brings pain, but it can also bring glory. It is short in terms of letters, but long in significance. This word has the power to turn a situation from bad to good, from wrong to right. The word I'm talking about is "no."

One of the major components to becoming successful and fulfilling your assignment in this world is your ability to focus. Laser-sharp focus is a direct result of properly using the word "no." We must all become familiar with and comfortable using this word at some point in our lives. Truth be told, the more you grow and mature as a person, the more opportunities you'll be faced with where you have to say "no." Warren Buffett says, "The difference between successful people and really successful people is that really successful people say no to almost everything."

As an athlete and a student, I understood the power of "no." But as a son, brother, friend, and husband, this word was foreign to me. The first day I learned to say "no" was heart-wrenching. It went against everything in my entire body. The sound of those two letters when used together rang in my ears for what seemed like an eternity. On a personal level, it was easy to use toward myself. There was nothing for me to sacrifice and go without. I could (and still) can say "no" to myself. But it was really hard for me to ask someone I loved to forgo something they desired, even when it was in their best interest. I would choose to deny myself first and give someone else something they didn't need rather than tell them "no" or expect them to sacrifice like I had sacrificed.

When I finally learned to start saying "no" to people I cared for deeply—which by the way has taken me a lifetime and I am still a work in progress—every fiber in my being resisted. It was dreadful, painful, and tortuous. But it had to be said for me to take full responsibility for my role in the process. Plus, I knew it was time for me to start saying "no," because it was the right thing to do. There's a big difference between doing what's good for you and doing what's right for you. Doing what's right may not always be the most popular or the most profitable choice, but it will always be the most prosperous.

There's a huge difference between doing something and doing something right. Before doing anything else, we should always strive to do what's right. What we say "no" to is just as important as what we say "yes" to. That's because when you say "yes" to one thing, you're also saying "no" to something else.

## Parents and Sacrifice

Parents sacrifice for their children. God made the greatest sacrifice of all when He sent His one and only Son to die for us on the cross. Jesus paid a debt He did not owe for a debt we could not pay. And He did it all for us, His children. He sacrificed out of love.

Hopefully, when we make these sacrifices, they are coming from a place of unconditional love. It's when we start determining how others, including our own children, should sacrifice for us, that we cross a line and set ourselves up for disappointment.

If you are working two jobs to support your family, or support your child's dream, I hope you are doing it because you want to. However, if you're keeping score for some future payday, or you have a hidden agenda, then you're rolling the dice, and there's a good chance your child might not make good on your investment. At the same time, it's entirely appropriate for a parent to require a child to also invest in their own dreams—to have some of their own "skin in the game," so to speak. This might look like chores, maintaining good grades, staying out of trouble, dedicating extra time to working on his or her craft, or even working a part-time job. As parents, the key is to check your heart and motivations to prevent or guard against any resentment creeping in against your child later on down the road.

## Testing Your Motives

The best and healthiest relationships—in marriage, friendship, or between a parent and their child—offer unconditional love and support. This is important, because in every kind of relationship, your motives will be tested. Imagine you have worked two jobs for years, skipped vacations, neglected your own desires, needs, and wants, and sacrificed to send your child to a private school in the hope that your child will earn a scholarship to a prestigious university. What if your child comes to you after their high school graduation ceremony and says, "Mom, Dad, I don't think college is for me. I want to get a job and stay at home." Or after three years in college, your child announces, "I don't want to go to school anymore. I think I'm gonna take some time off for myself and travel the world." What would your reaction be? Honestly, how would that make you feel? What would you do right before you proceeded to choke them? Pray, I hope! (Of course, I am only joking about the choking.)

The real question, however, should be, what are your expectations for your child? Have you made your expectations known to your child, and do they line up with your child's expectations for themselves? And, whose dream was it for them to go to college and get a degree? Was it more or all about you and not about them? (I am guilty as charged. I taught my kids the Florida State Seminole war chant before they learned how to spell their own names.)

We all play a role in setting, and in responding to, misplaced expectations. Once you open the can of worms, also known as expectations, the expectations spread quickly and start to work both ways. Yes, both ways. So, let's talk about a parent and child relationship that is healthy. How do you help a child buy into both the glory and the pain of a dream without superimposing your own expectations on them? How do you make them realize that anything in life worth having is also worth working hard for? And lastly, what can you do to make your child understand that nothing in life is free? These days, it's rare to find free water and bread. And, if they are truly free, it's probably best you don't partake in them. There are only a few places that come to mind where I know you can find free food: a garbage can, in a mousetrap, and on the end of a fishing hook. Last time I checked, none of these ended well for the discoverer.

There is no elevator to success. Everyone must eventually use the stairs. Of course, the escalator will be more comfortable, but it will also be more crowded. There's rarely any traffic on that extra mile or going the hard way. If you insist on using the escalator, walk up the side that's going down. This will illustrate to you how hard you must work and how you can't stop working until you get all the way to the top. And then, you must work even harder to stay there.

We can't just sit in our recliner and expect others to feed us. In scripture, Paul reinforces this notion when he writes in 2 Thessalonians 3:10, "For even when we were with you, we commanded you this: If anyone will not work, neither shall he eat." My parents and grandparents sketched this truth on my forehead in blood as a child. And what they failed to mention to me, my ordained coaches throughout my playing career shared. Phrases that quickly come to mind include:

- "No guts, no glory!"
- "No pain, no gain!"
- "You get out what you put in!"
- "Hard work beats talent when talent doesn't work hard!"
- "Do the work others aren't willing to do, and you'll get the results others will never have!"

What a great way to start this tough conversation with your kids. There is nothing wrong with them hearing it from you first. Parents should put some of the onus of responsibility on the child. The only reason I could play sports was because I made good grades, I stayed out of trouble, and I was totally committed. The minute my attitude or actions did not reflect any of that, privileges were taken from me, with no explanation whatsoever.

Playing sports in my house was not a necessity or a mandate, it was a privilege. My parents and I had a shared agreement or unwritten contract that had clear expectations. My dad spent countless hours driving me to and from practices and games, both football and basketball, for years. I loved playing, and he loved supporting me. His only rules were I needed to maintain my grades, stay out of trouble, respect my coaches the same way I respected him, compete hard, avoid being lazy, and, once I started a season, I could not quit, no matter what. Simple, right?

## Parents and Pain

When I was in eighth grade, our football team went 6-0 and won the city conference championship. We did something special and unprecedented by going undefeated and unscored on for the entire season. It's something that has not been repeated to this day. As the football season ended, it was off to the basketball courts for me. Picking up right where we left off on the gridiron, our basketball team also won the city conference championship, losing only two games the entire season. We were preparing to play in our conference championship game when my life changed.

The gym was overflowing with kids, parents, teachers, as well as middle school players and coaches from the surrounding area. Even the high school coaches and several of the high school players were there, getting a preview of what the next generation of local stars looked like. They all wanted to see what all the fuss was about this Chris Hope kid that had the entire city raving. The announcer began to call out the starting lineups for both teams. We were the top seed in the tournament and also the home team, so he introduced my team last. It was so loud and crazy in the gym, we could barely hear whose name was being called next. I was normally the last player introduced, so I was still rather relaxed and zoned out. After the announcer called my last teammate's name, I started to tuck in my jersey. The minute I stood up, the cheers got louder, and the gym erupted.

As I ran to high-five my teammates, I felt a tug on my jersey. We were just kids and always full of jokes. So, I thought for sure one of my friends was trying to be funny and maybe trying to pull my shorts down before I ran out. Now that, in itself, would have been an unforgettable moment. So, without looking back, I tried to slap what I thought to be my teammate's hand away. But this was no ordinary middle school kid's grip.

I turned around and was shocked to see my dad standing there. It still amazes me to this day how loud and crazy it was in the gym that night. But, at that very moment, I could hear the whisper of a church mouse. It was almost as if someone were playing a video game and accidentally pushed the pause button. I heard my dad loud and clear, but I could not believe his words: "Come on. You are going home." I was stunned. "Going home?' What do you mean I'm going home?" I yelled. "You are not playing tonight," he said sternly. "But it's the championship game, what do you mean I'm not playing?" "You are not playing. End of discussion. Now, come on."

I looked to my coach in a state of desperation as he walked over to see what was going on. My dad was polite but firm. "This is my son, and I'm not explaining it to you, and I'm definitely not explaining it to him. He's just not playing tonight. You're going to have to play and win it without him tonight, Coach." With that, my dad walked off the court and headed toward the exit. As he started to walk, he said without looking back, "Chris, don't make me have to turn around again." I was in disbelief and had no idea what just happened—or why. Can you imagine the anger, the disappointment, the embarrassment, the frustration, and the pain I was experiencing?

I can still remember the drive home like it was yesterday. We were in my dad's old black Chevy pickup truck, the one that had the bench seat in the front. My brother, who on any other night would have fought me over the window seat, sat in between my dad and me. He must have felt the rage and steam coming off my body. We left the gym so quickly, I didn't even get a chance to go back to the locker room to change back into my school clothes or to get my books for class the next day.

I wanted and needed answers. Throughout my childhood and young adult life, I never talked back to my dad, questioned my dad, or antagonized my dad. I just remember him saying, "Chris, leave it alone." But, I was so angry I couldn't let it go, so I kept asking, "What did I do wrong?" As I continued to ask questions, my brother kept nudging me, which back then translated into, *"Please, let it go, man. Tonight is not the night. Nothing is going to work."*

As we pulled into our driveway, the nightmare that I thought I would soon wake up from became a harsh reality. In complete silence, we all got out of the truck, went into the house, and went into our separate rooms. And no one said another word the rest of the night. Heading to my room still boiling hot, I walked through our main living space where we had a big wall-sized mirror hanging, and I couldn't help but notice I still had my entire uniform on: tights, game socks, wristbands, and my jersey, still untucked. At that very moment, it felt like all the emotions I experienced earlier hit me all over again. This time, however, they hit me all at once.

I was embarrassed. I was hurt. I was angry. I was depressed. I was disappointed. You name any negative emotion, and I was feeling it. I let my team down. I let my coaches down. I let my school down. I let my city down. But most importantly, I let myself down. And I felt like whatever I had done couldn't have been that bad.

I found out later, just as my dad and brother were leaving the house to come watch my game, the phone rang. Oddly enough, my brother decided to answer the phone. It was one of my teachers, calling to inform my parents about my disruptive behavior that day in school. And just to show how small our town is, it was a teacher who also taught my dad and my brother when they were younger—Miss West. I was upset with her for a long time after that. I didn't talk to her or speak in her class for at least a month. We lost the game that night. And to be completely honest, that night I lost some love for the first love of my life, basketball.

I was furious at my dad and at my brother that night. But I probably learned more from that game, or missed game, than from any other experience in my life thus far. As a result of that painful event, I learned that at any given moment your dreams could be all over. They could be snatched right out from under you. There were no guarantees in sports—or in life. And after that day, I believed my dad whenever he said, "You are going to do it my way or not at all." I had bought in completely and never had another problem after that. Through the pain, I understood the glory—at least, I understood it a bit more. And it changed my approach to sports and life throughout my career.

## Parents Providing

I can honestly say, as a kid playing sports, my parents were not driven by money. My parents' commitment and involvement in my sports career was not based on this idea of finding a pot of gold on the other side my career. Instead, they were motivated by one desire—the development of my character. My dad was not worried about who won the championship game, how many touchdowns or points I scored, or if one day I would earn a scholarship or a professional contract. Like any good parent, he was more concerned with me becoming a good man.

It was a legacy decision on his part. That is why his decision that night, of not allowing me to play in the championship game, holds so much weight and has had such a significant impact on my life. It was his opportunity to not only get my undivided attention, but also his desire to teach me never to take anything for granted and to show me how one bad decision can cost me my destiny that truly grabbed me. I learned there was pain before the glory. And I had a part to play in the matter. If a professional sports career was what I wanted, then I had to put some "skin in the game." I not only had to prove it to myself; I also had to convince my parents every day that this was the type of life I both desired and deserved.

The experience of not being able to play in that championship game jolted me and tarnished my love for the game of basketball. However, now that I'm all grown up, I fully understand why my father did what he did, and I can't blame him or be mad at anyone but myself. At the end of the day, it was a blessing in disguise. After that incident, I realized every opportunity I had to play any game I loved, I had to play it like it could be my last game. Also, at that point, I decided to focus more on football. So, in the end, it all worked out for my highest good.

Your responsibility as a parent is to provide for your kids. That doesn't mean providing everything they think they want. It means providing what they really need. And there is a big difference between the two. As a child, your parents may not buy you the most expensive shoes, and you might not even have a closet with several pairs of shoes in it to choose from. But I am more than positive that your parents, another family member, or a friend would be willing to assist you with at least one pair of shoes to wear.

An old man once shared a story with me that I've never forgotten. It has always held a special place in my heart. It has helped me stay grounded throughout my life and sports career. The story was about two men who both had an issue—a very legitimate condition. But, one chose to complain while the other chose to rejoice. The first man complained and fussed about not having any shoes to wear, and he exclaimed to every person he met how God did not love him. Until, he met the other man who did not have any shoes to wear and, more importantly, was born without feet. We must learn to be thankful and grateful for what we have, no matter how good or bad we think our situation is.

We all must take full responsibility for our current situations. Just like we should be willing to step up to the plate and take control of our dreams. Your home may not have nine bedrooms. Instead, it may be a modest apartment. But, at least you have a roof over your head. So, be content and grateful for what you have in your life, but don't become complacent or grow comfortable where you are. Your parents may not be able to afford to send you to Yale, or Florida State, but you can always build on your education. You can do this by working harder, reading more, studying longer, and earning your own scholarship to whatever college you wish to attend. Then, one day you will be able to buy the house of your dreams.

Isn't it funny how we tend to put high expectations on what others should do for us and low expectations on what we should do for ourselves? And isn't it sad how we have similar expectations on others about how they should spend their own money? What screws up most of us in life is the picture we've painted in our minds of how things are supposed to be.

## Saying "No"

When I was informed in 2009 that I had been selected to the Pro Bowl team, I experienced so many different emotions. I was anxious, excited, grateful, humbled, overjoyed, proud, and relieved. I thought to myself, *"Wow, all that hard work finally paid off."* I also felt extremely torn, because I had a big decision to make regarding a goal I had set for myself. In life, we should all make goals for ourselves. And we should not just make goals, we should also write them down. As Fitzhugh Dodson said, "Goals that are not written down are just wishes."

That previous off-season was a different one for me. In fact, as I think about it now, it was the only off-season of my long career that I had the challenge of bouncing back from a serious injury. So, I challenged myself to come back stronger, faster, tougher, and in the best shape of my life. I vowed this would be the best season of my career and that I would give my all to make the Pro Bowl. I had a tough hill to climb and a lot of work to do, but I was devoted. If I accomplished my goal at the end of the season, my incentive, or gift to myself, was going to be an exotic, top-of-the-line luxury car. I'd narrowed it down to either a Bentley, a Rolls-Royce, or a Lamborghini. In my mind, that car was my reward. But, when the time came, I could not convince myself to sign on the dotted line. I thought about some of my family and friends who I knew were struggling. *How could I drive around in a $400,000 car when I knew these people needed help?* I had an internal battle over this decision for months.

In the end, I am glad I didn't buy that car! Not because I thought I didn't deserve it, but because the situation challenged me to look at my motivations differently and to remember what was most important to me. It's important to be generous, but we must define generosity for ourselves, in our own ways. I'd seen my friends in the NFL bail out many of their friends and family members over the years, and the situations of those they helped did not change. Instead of using the help to improve their situations, they expected to be rescued repeatedly and failed to take responsibility for their own dreams. So, I realized if I bought my dream car or not, those same people I had sympathy for were not going to change or be affected by my decision. I came to the conclusion that it was not about how they felt or what they thought about me if I had a nicer car. Instead, it was all about how it would have made me feel. And, at the time, I just couldn't do it.

I know that it's difficult to say no to the people we love. I can't imagine what it took for my dad to pull me out of that championship game. How he must have resented me for putting him in that tough position in the first place. But that's what made me appreciate, and not take for granted, my opportunities later on when I faced adversity. It's what it took to make me a champion. Or rather, what it took to make me step up and become my own champion.

When you begin to experience success, on the field or off,

people's expectations of you, and about you, start to change. Even the expectations of your family and close friends. Trust me when I tell you this: You won't see it coming. You'll be surprised and shocked to see who shows their hand first. I experienced this firsthand. As a result, my circle has gotten a lot smaller over the years. I'm just glad that, in life, when dealing with certain issues, less is more.

It's so important for you to learn how to and find the resolve to say "no" when there are unhealthy expectations. When a receiver steps out of bounds, the quarterback should not pass the ball to him. It would be a wasted play. When family and friends start telling you how to live your life and suggesting what they would do if they were you, they, too, are out of bounds. When this happens, boldly and respectfully put them in their places. Do not overlook it or sweep it under the rug. If you do that, it will just sit and wait for the next opportunity to come out and pollute the atmosphere. And when people try to get between the decisions you and your spouse make together, that's a major interference. Again, respectfully address the situation immediately. You must set the tone often and early, or the tone will be set for you—and on you.

Real sacrifice, the kind that is based on unconditional love, gives without expectation of return. And it says "no" when that's the right answer. When you sacrifice something you desire, love, or want, you're not losing this thing. Instead, you're giving it away or passing it on to someone else so they can be blessed.

If you haven't had this realization yet, you will soon come to understand that there will *always* be a need. That's why it's so critical that you learn to manage the blessings you have been entrusted with. What I had to learn, and what I hope you will also find helpful, is how to recognize when others were placing their expectations on me—and how to confidently say "no." Once you have said "no," stand by it. Remember, those who ask (and receive what they ask you for) never question why you said "yes." They will gladly accept your generosity and continue on with their day. So, why do we feel like we have to explain our "nos"? At some point, we all must make a hard choice. Who will you listen to when this happens?

# TURNOVERS

- Feeling like you always should say "yes" to everything that is asked of you.
- Being distracted by things that have nothing to do with your goals.
- When you sacrifice your own happiness for the sake of someone else but hold them hostage for your decision to do so.

# TAKEAWAYS

- Learn to say "no." You don't have to explain your "yes," so don't feel obligated to explain whenever you say "no."
- Make sure your sacrifices are from your heart and that they don't have any strings or hidden agendas attached to them.
- Encourage your loved ones (parents/siblings) or child to put some of their own "skin in the game" and then hold them accountable.

# Chapter 5

# RICHES VERSUS WEALTH

True wealth is not something I see very often in my community or culture. I strongly believe wealth is so much deeper than what's in someone's checking account, savings account, 401(k), retirement fund, or buried in their backyard. And if you're old-school or born into a provincial family like mine, your wealth may just be secretly tucked under a mattress or hidden away in a barn somewhere.

Believe it or not, when I looked up the meaning of the word "wealth," the word "money" was rarely used. Sure, money is a significant part of the equation, but it is far from being the only measure when determining if a person is wealthy or not. I did, however, find several other words—such as "abundance," "affluence," "assets," "fortune," "influence," "plentiful," "prosperity," "resources," "substance," and "value"—that were used to describe wealth.

I'll go even deeper and share what I believe true wealth is. First and foremost, the greatest wealth a person can have is wisdom and good health. Without these two, the third one, which is money, is useless. Wealth to me is all of these things. However, without the proper mind-set and education, no matter how much money a person has, they can still be poor. The world is filled with two types of people: a lot of poor, rich people, and a lot of rich, poor people. And, in my experience, the difference between the two has everything to do with mind-set and education, not a pay stub. How do you like that for an oxymoron?

The great American philosopher and psychologist William James stated, "The greatest discovery of any generation is that a human being can alter his life by changing his attitude." In Psalm 66:12, the Bible states that God brought the people out of bondage and turmoil into a wealthy place. I truly believe that God wants us all to arrive at a place of wealth. So, no matter what our state of living is, we'll never have a poor person's mentality or spirit of lack, regardless of our ability to access natural or human resources, because we know who our *one* true source and provider is. Our connection to God is critical to our survival. The enemy's plan isn't always to cause bodily harm to us, but rather to disconnect us from our source. Thus, we must learn to stay connected to the source and not focus so much on being connected to the resource.

Chris Rock, during one of his many stand-up comedy shows, told a joke that provoked my lack of understanding and knowledge on the difference between being rich versus being wealthy. Not only did he enlighten me, he also ignited a fire in my bones. He talked about how several black people, mostly athletes and entertainers, across the country have been blessed and fortunate enough to become very successful, rich, and famous. But, he also shared how none of these same black people have managed to become wealthy. Rock said, "Shaq is rich," referring to NBA superstar Shaquille O'Neal, "but the white man who signs his checks is wealthy. Oprah is rich, but Bill Gates is wealthy. If Bill Gates suddenly woke up with Oprah's money, he'd slit his throat." Now, we all know and understand that was a joke and not 100 percent factual, due to the likes of Oprah and Shaq being two of the most recognizable black billionaires and multimillionaires. However, I completely understood the point or punchline of his joke.

## Instant Millionaires

Sure, we have people around us who become rich, especially in my profession. Being drafted into a professional sport, depending on what round you are drafted in or how high you are selected, can be just like winning the lottery. Literally, you can become an instant millionaire in a matter of seconds, depending on how long it takes the commissioner to say your name. Before my NFL draft day, I remember being interviewed by a psychologist who worked for the San Francisco 49ers. This interview occurred when I was at the NFL Scouting Combine, a place where college football players perform physical and mental tests in front of NFL coaches, general managers, and scouts. Right before I walked out of the door, the doctor said, "The night of the draft, spend time with your family, go watch a movie, or take the family out to grab a bite to eat. Don't stress yourself out by watching the draft. Just know that whenever your name is called, you will be a much richer man than you were before they called your name." I wasn't fortunate enough to be a first-rounder or a really high draft pick, but no matter what round I went in, what the psychologist said was very true. The definition of "rich" actually depended on my mind-set.

The truth of the matter was this. I really was going to be richer than I was the night before I went to sleep. However, pay close attention. He said "richer," not wealthier. This is where the lack of education comes into play. So many people are misinformed by what they hear, see on TV, or what they assume to be true. All athletes who are drafted, or who are blessed enough to make the roster of any professional sports team, do not automatically become rich and "set for life." It also does not mean that the athlete can hit the relax button and put the plane in autopilot and coast on home as if all the work has been done. It just means that the athlete will now be earning a good salary for what he or she has been doing their entire life, which means it's much bigger than a game . . . it's now a J-O-B.

This also holds true in the entertainment and business

worlds as well as in many different medical professions. Just because you have letters in front of your name, a hit song playing on the radio, or a major role in a movie, doesn't mean it's time to buy your retirement home on the beach. As an individual begins to embark on this new journey on the highest level in their profession, it's no different than any other promotion in life. The commitment, demands, pressure, problems, responsibilities, stress, and workload will all increase for the person as they tackle their new position. It's not time for anyone, especially family and close friends, to rest and relax. And we all know the athlete, or the talent, can't stop working. In fact, they must work harder than they ever have before. It's not the time to put your life in "Neutral" or "Park." No different than the athlete, we as a family have to find a way to shift into a higher gear, because there's always so much more work to be done. It's time to dig deeper and work harder, collectively.

## Jump Aboard

When your life is blessed in this way, something strange happens. We can all agree and expect that the life of the person who has just been blessed with money and opportunity will change to some degree. However, the real surprise and shocker is how much change you'll see in the people *surrounding* the person who has just walked into this new way of living. It's very comparable to a parasitic relationship in which one organism, the parasite, lives off another organism, the host, harming it and possibly causing death. Instead of catching inspiration or using what they've witnessed as motivation in their own lives, they choose to jump off their own path and jump on the rich person's surfboard until it brings everyone down.

You'll quickly find out that some people are connected to you while others are *attached* to you. Those connected to you don't need a warranty. But you'll want to keep all your receipts and have your photo ID handy for those who are attached to you. Trust me when I say this: One day you'll surely need to repair them, replace them, or completely erase them. Those connected to you are of great value and substance; whereas, those attached to you are valueless and deficient. Their commitment to you is only contingent upon what you can give them or do for them. The minute you can no longer give them what they desire will also be the minute they no longer remain committed to you. Money attracts a circle of dependents. The more cheese, or money, you have, the more rats you attract. When all the cheese is gone, you'll mysteriously no longer have a rat problem.

Where there is success in any profession in the black community, there's an unwritten motto or tradition of, "When one of us makes it, we all make it." And we all know what that means. Everyone quits working, while the one who "makes it" must work even harder to not only increase his or her new workload but also to take care of those who have just became their new dependents. Everyone just sits back in the shade, while the "cash cow" is drained emotionally, financially, mentally, physically, and spiritually. The dependent's individual dreams, goals, and motivations stopped the minute their loved one's dreams became a reality. Can someone please help me make some sense out of that? Why do they sit back and watch the cash cow kill himself? Instead, why not call forth new waves and create a tsunami of success as a family?

## God Funds Purpose

To me, that's the difference between being rich and being wealthy. In the simplest form, riches are short-term monies that expire during one generation or less due to unaltered mind-sets and a lack of education and vision. Being rich consists of owning material things, mostly depreciating assets, with little to no value. Being rich is based solely on having a lot of money and an accumulation of stuff. But, without having a purpose behind it, the idea of going broke will always lie dormant in the back of their minds.

Whereas, being wealthy entails having long-term financial staying power that's so immense it can be passed down through generations. When you are wealthy, you have investments, land, networks, opportunities, education, a mind-set of abundance, some depreciating assets (but mostly appreciating assets), and a reciprocal relationship with God. Having wealth also means having a lot of money, but, unlike having riches, when you have wealth, there is a purpose and a vision behind the money. Wealthy people use their resources and money beyond themselves. When we're not willing to give anything, we end up risking everything. Master Choa Kok Sui says, "The soul grows by giving, not by accumulating!"

God funds purpose, but He does not fund pleasure. That's why those who are living "in purpose" never go broke. Money with purpose is powerful. Money without purpose is just a bunch of zeros and commas that will sooner, rather than later, run out. Personally, I want to be wealthy, rather than just see one generation, or one family, get rich. I want to create a legacy that others can be born into—and inherit.

Rich people acquire stuff, while wealthy people acquire power. See the difference?

## Imagine True Wealth

It's one thing to imagine your own success, but have you ever imagined your grandchildren being born into a wealthy family? I know many of us don't look that far down the road, but when God blesses us, or gives us an assignment, it's never just only for us. It's always meant to bless and help others. We never experience true success until we learn how to serve others. When we give of ourselves to help others, especially those in life who can't bless us back, we can't help but be rewarded. To me, that's true wealth. Blessing someone isn't a debt we owe, but a seed we sow.

My granddaughters and grandsons are already millionaires, even though they have yet to be born. I believe that what we don't see, we don't get. That's why I choose to dream about the legacy I am leaving to my grandchildren every night and speak that declaration over them. That's one of the goals my wife and I have set for our family.

When we speak, it's no different than when God speaks. Our words should always be on assignment, because God's word never returns void. What we hear will always be greater than what we see. If you're a person who must see before you believe, you'll always arrive at your place of destiny late. I know this is a major contradiction from what we were taught growing up, but we should adopt the new mind-set of believing when we hear it and not having to wait to see it, especially when spoken by God. If we hear better, we'll start to think better. When we start to think better, we'll start to speak better. When we start to speak better, we'll finally start to do better.

As King Solomon said in Proverbs 13:22, "A good man leaves an inheritance to his children's children." This verse made me think and ask myself several questions: What's the definition of inheritance? Is inheritance only limited to money or possessions? Is it better to pass down opportunity rather than wealth alone? What was King Solomon referring to when he spoke this word?

I believe inheritance isn't just about what you leave behind for someone. It's also, and more importantly, what you leave *in* someone's heart: spiritual beliefs, discipline, positive habits, knowledge, strong morals, good relationships, solid values, and a good work ethic. Now that I'm older and have children of my own, that's what I feel like Solomon was referencing. Inheritance, just like wealth, is so much more than money. "There is much more to wealth than simply a bank account with many zeros. A well-balanced, whole life is made up of wealth and success that come from many facets; family, friends, work, faith, it's the complete person who works on each of these areas and creates the whole," says Celso Cukierkorn in his landmark book, *Secrets of Jewish Wealth Revealed!* I'm not talking about stereotypical kids with trust funds who never learn to study or work and receive a fat check every month once they turn twenty-one. Those kids might be rich, but they aren't necessarily wealthy.

Wealthy people create value. Wealthy people are givers, not takers. Wealthy families create a legacy. And they never quit. They hold each future generation accountable for playing their role in sustaining and adding their own unique worth to the family. As parents who want to leave a legacy, but might not be fortunate enough to "make it" financially, we must have the mind-set that we'll keep working, giving, teaching, creating value, and being a good example for our children to model, even if they succeed beyond our wildest dreams.

Material success can be fleeting, but a legacy of wealth must be built and taught from one generation to another, if it plans to stand the test of time. And we, as parents, should be committed to building our legacies by our own example. For example, why, as a parent, can you not continue to work until you choose to retire, or, better yet, when you're at the eligible age to retire? Don't leave all that money on the table you've worked so hard for all those years. Why quit your job when you're still young, healthy, productive, and able to take care of yourself to only become totally dependent on your child whose life is just beginning? Why stop living your own life, only to start living your child's life? No matter how successful or financially blessed our children become, Linda and I will keep building a legacy by our example. By continuing to work and provide for ourselves, we'll be assisting our children in paying it forward and not hindering them. We won't prevent them from being able to fully grow and focus on their own lives and families. We'll still be very important to them, but we'll also work to not be their focal point.

Any time our children choose to bless my wife and I with something, it will only be overflow or icing on the cake for us. When they do this, we want it to truly be something they want to do for us from the bottom of their hearts, not because they need or have to or because we are in dire need of it and wouldn't be able to survive without it. The only way to avoid disappointment is by never expecting anything. The bigger our expectations are, the bigger our disappointments will be.

I always envisioned my own parents would continue to do some type of work until they couldn't anymore. The work wouldn't be strenuous or stressful. Instead, it would be something to keep them active, sharp, and alive. It wouldn't necessarily be for them to pay their bills or make ends meet. Instead, them working would solely be so that they can save and have their own money to live and enjoy life the way they want to and have always dreamed of. I want them to be able to fulfill their imaginations and desires and not worry if they have enough money to eat, keep their lights on, pay their mortgage, or keep up with their house and car taxes. I don't want them to have to sit around and wait for me to make a phone call or put money into their accounts before they can do something they enjoy. Instead, I want them to be able to travel the world or at least come visit or send for their grandkids without waiting for me to make it happen for them. They shouldn't have to wait for me to give them money and then turn right back around and buy me a Christmas or birthday gift with the money I sent. I mean, there is some good in that, I guess. They could've chosen not to celebrate me even after giving them the money. (See how I am taking my own advice and attempting to find the good in everything?)

Even though Linda and I make money through ventures we have started since I retired from the NFL, we also have dreams of doing bigger and better things. But if I'm constantly giving it out to support other family members and friends, how can we plan for our kid's inheritance? Take the extreme example of an NHL hockey player filing for bankruptcy in 2014, while earning a five-million dollar per year salary! Reportedly the player's family members, who had power of attorney over his finances, racked up a huge debt to finance an elaborate lifestyle.[1] Yes, success is meant to be shared. But, those who can provide for themselves, should do so and build their own life legacy.

## But I Hate My Job

Some of you might be thinking, *yeah, Chris, that's easy for you to say. You've made it. But I'm stuck here.* This might apply to you, or your friends and family. So, let's tackle this issue head-on.

Success usually has one of two effects on people: energy or envy. Envy comes from a mind-set of lack and self-doubt. Sometimes, it sounds something like: *Wow, she made it. I need some of what she has.* Or: *I sacrificed to help them get there, so now they owe me something.* Or: *She is living the life I was supposed to live. Why is that not me instead of her? I was better and smarter than her. How did she make it instead of me?*

Energy, on the other hand, comes when others are motivated when they see someone succeed. It might sound like: *Wow, she went after her dream, took some risks, and worked hard. I can do that! If anyone in the world deserves it, it has to be her, because I watched her put in the work. I am truly happy for her, because she was focused and did not allow anything to get in the way of accomplishing her dreams.*

Bishop Walker always says that "people that are truly happy for you, celebrate you whether your success or happiness ben-

---

1. http://bluejacketsxtra.dispatch.com/content/stories/2016/11/12/blue-jackets--jack-johnson-gives-up-most-of-2-years-pay-in-bankruptcy-settlement.html

efits them or not. If they are only happy for you when it bene-fits them, they aren't celebrating you. They are only tolerating you." Along these lines, if you give an envious person $10,000, they will probably head to the mall to buy everything they already saw you purchase. But, if you give an energized person the money, they'll invest in their dream.

When God gives you a vision, you must be the first one to invest in, or act on, your vision. In addition to acting on your vision, your life must be in order and in proper alignment with God. No one puts money in a vending machine that has an "Out of Order" sign on it. If you're not willing to help yourself, don't expect anyone else to do so either.

Generosity and wisdom must come together to help us make sound financial decisions as they relate to helping friends and family. Being the "chosen one" has its perks, but it also has its disadvantages. Celso Cukierkorn states, "Arrogance is knowledge minus wisdom." He says this because if you only have knowledge or skill, such as an athletic skill, without the humility that comes with wisdom, disaster is just around the corner.

I never had a safety net. It was all on me—sink or swim. My family didn't have much money, but they worked hard. And they had wisdom. I learned the value of a dollar and saw what hard work and dedication looked like firsthand. My parent's legacy built a strong work ethic in me, and it's impossible to put a price tag on that. There are times when providing a safety net for someone can be a real game changer. It can either motivate and assist a person or make them lazy and handicap them to the point they lack desire, drive, and passion. It all depends on whether or not they have a legacy mind-set. One of the most difficult parts about being a leader is getting someone to buy into what you're saying and to change their mind-set. Moses struggled back and forth with the Pharaoh to let his people go from Egypt, only to find himself later wrestling with his own people to let go of Egypt. I can relate to this story. In my family, we have been long gone from Saluda Street, but Saluda Street has never left us.

## Why Not?

You might be successful and wondering about how to help others. Or you might be struggling, looking for the support of others. No matter what your situation is, my question and challenge are still the same: Why aren't you going after your own dreams and building your own legacy? Parents, I'm talking about living independently from your child's success. Here is an easy tip to start your journey to becoming successful and making an effective change in your life: Let go of whatever is stopping you. If you are finding that challenging, ask God to disconnect you from harmful distractions.

Once you figure out your *why*, you'll be able to overcome your *why not*. Maybe you're like me in terms of being new to financial success. I wasn't accustomed to the experience of having more money than I needed to pay the rent. And I made plenty of mistakes trying to figure it out. Today, I'm still making mistakes and figuring things out. When you come from money, your parents can tell you how to handle riches or prepare you for it, and you'll hopefully learn from their example. But, when you're the first generation of financial success, there are no guidelines. You simply learn from the mistakes of others. That's one of the main reasons this book exists. I wrote it to help others navigate the road to true peace, success, and wealth.

## Higher Thinking

Riches are strictly monetary. Wealth, however, is so much more. It all starts and ends with your mind-set—just like the story of the man who was angry because he had no shoes, until he met the man who had no feet. Suddenly, the shoeless man felt wealthy. Change is never about a matter of ability. It's always about a matter of circumstance and motivation. Mind-set changes everything.

Having the opportunity to participate in many different sports growing up, I was exposed to, and surrounded by, many people with different types of personalities, backgrounds, gifts, and talents. I was blessed and fortunate enough to play with, and be coached by, some amazing people—truly gifted and exceptionally talented people.

One characteristic that helped me become successful on every level was my ability to model other people's best practices. No matter who the person was, what position they played, how old they were, or if they were a starter on the team or not, if they did something that could make me a better person or a more complete player, I watched them and learned how to do it. In other words, I put it in my "game." Steven Silbiger says in *The Jewish Phenomenon* that Jewish Americans are, as a group, the wealthiest ethnic group in America. They have figured it out. They have cracked the code, and they have continued to share it with each other for centuries. This is why I decided to study the Jewish culture and their practices when it comes to wealth.

The Jewish culture has a tradition of passing wealth down from one generation to the next. This is expected. And it's a very good expectation. Expectations form mind-sets and world-views—and endless possibilities. The by-product of this culture is not only material wealth, but also a wealthy mind-set. In thinking and living this way, they not only help each other financially, they also, most importantly, help each other mentally. They don't give back to their families and communities. Instead, they invest in their families and communities. And they don't invest in addictions and desires. They invest in change.

Let me be clear. I'm not against gifting to people I love, at times. It's an amazing feeling to be able to bless someone. But a gift is something given voluntarily to someone without expecting to receive anything in return. When you invest in someone or something, there's an expectation of a worthwhile result.

The worthwhile result isn't necessarily directed toward the investor. Instead, there is an expectation to bring value to the one that's been invested in. Then everyone can swim for themselves.

The Jewish culture believes the best possible investment a person can make in their future is in their education. Gaining knowledge for knowledge's sake is a core Jewish value. Knowledge is a natural magnet for wealth. That's why education is their number one goal. They see having a great education as the great equalizer for everyone. You can take away someone's riches, but if they have a wealthy mind-set and a good knowledge base, they'll figure out a new way to regain their riches and enjoy the journey doing so. As Ali ibn Abi-Talib once said, "There is no wealth like knowledge and no poverty like ignorance."

## Who Will You Listen To?

The pressure, responsibility, and stress of being the first generation to have financial success is immeasurable. And the weight of protecting your financial success is even heavier. True success is not only measured by someone becoming wealthy and famous, it's also about being able to sustain it, maintain it, grow it, share it, and be a good steward of it. Among financial advisors, there's an old saying: "The first generation makes it, the second generation enjoys it, and the third generation blows it."

I've seen communities, families, and friends help speed up the process of turning success into failure—from the first to get rich to the first to go broke. Then, to add insult to injury, they turn and point their fingers at the successful person for being unwise about their financial decision-making.

Saving the hood or gaining street credit isn't the best way of showing your loyalty or love for someone. Just look at the financial ruin of people like MC Hammer, Mike Tyson, Allen Iverson, and Antoine Walker. They all had help spending their riches and, in turn, they had help going broke. But, they're the only ones who received all the blame and shame for it. At the end of the day, as sad as it sounds and as bad as it hurts for me to say this, they were ultimately responsible for how they stewarded their finances.

I'm the first to admit that I've sometimes been guilty of giving for the wrong reasons. And in the process, I could've lost a tremendous opportunity to build a legacy for my children, grandchildren, and generations beyond. In the past, I saw my blessings as a vehicle for what I wanted to do for others, instead of listening to how God instructed me to bless people. Often, I didn't wait for the counsel of God. I just acted out of emotion, fear, or guilt. However, when it comes to enjoying true wealth, we create the standard. We must decide who we'll listen to. We can make ourselves feel responsible for paying others' bills, paying off family members' debts, buying outrageous Christmas presents, and even giving jobs. The list goes on and on.

I've always had the attitude of trying to win every game. My approach never changed, but the results sometimes did. Even when you lose, you can have winning and teachable moments that help decrease your chances of losing again. It's better to fail at something than to excel at nothing. Learn the lessons from your mistakes and forget the details. Remember, the call is always higher than the fall.

On the football field, my coaches always had the utmost confidence in me to make the play if no one else would. I was always the last line of defense—my team's last hope. I took that responsibility seriously and was smart and fast enough to cover the entire field on every play. I also took that same approach in my life, but what I didn't take into account was that life isn't played on a 100-yard football field. And, on any given day, there are way more than ten people for me to try to cover for. I've learned that I can't do it all. I never could. And I must choose.

Jesus didn't perform miracles everywhere he went or for every person in need. So, why are you and I trying to? When you understand that wealth is different than mere riches, you can focus on building wealth in your family for generations to come. As a result, we'll stop living rich and dying broke—be it financially, spiritually, or emotionally.

# TURNOVERS

- Don't allow or influence your loved ones to quit their jobs to become your dependents or responsibility.
- Don't put your life in autopilot because you have become rich. Money without purpose or vision will run out. Like the adage says, "A fool and money will soon part ways."
- Don't allow guilt and fear to prevent you from building a legacy for your children and future generations.
- The higher the level of expectations, the higher the level of disappointments will be.

# TAKEAWAYS

- We must not just give to our loved ones. Instead, we must learn to invest in them. Fund change, not addiction.
- A great education is true wealth. Without knowledge and the proper mind-set, no matter if you're rich or wealthy, your resources won't last.
- Inheritance isn't just what we leave for someone; it's also what we leave in someone.
- Parents and family members, pursue your own dreams. Don't stop living your lives or give up on your dreams to live through your child or loved ones.

## Chapter 6

# ASSIGNMENT VERSUS ASSUMPTION

So much of what makes us successful in life is learning what is necessary as opposed to what is expected. Another way to say this is to learn the difference between assignment and assumption. When it comes to assignment and assumption, improper use or misinterpretation of these two words can result in two different conclusions. One will make a fool out of you; whereas, the other can leave you slap dead in the middle of some serious you-know-what.

People are often pulled off course, because they either don't know their purpose in life, or they know their purpose but somehow lose sight of it. Many of us are distracted by engaging in activities that have nothing to do with our assignments, goals, and purposes. Yet, it's imperative that we find a way to starve our distractions and overfeed our focus.

My great friend and mentor Bishop Walker often reminds

his congregation, "If it's not a part of your assignment, then why is it on your calendar?" One of the world's greatest inventors and pioneers in the technology of our generation—former Apple CEO Steve Jobs—often said, "Deciding what not to do is as important as deciding what to do."

Pause for a moment, think about your schedule, and then ask yourself: *How do the two statements above affect or impact my life?* We all have our own individual crosses to bear, but many of us voluntarily pick up other people's crosses while continuing to carry our own. Consequently, we end up not completing our own assignments, because we assume the responsibilities of others. This leaves us angry, bitter, frustrated, tired, and full of resentment toward that person.

The "burning bush" in Exodus 3:2-3 depicts how our assignments from God should create a burning desire in our hearts but not burn us out. When God gives us an assignment, He also equips us with the skill set, mental capacity, physical ability, and discipline to be able to complete the assignment. He never gives us or puts more on us than we can handle or bear. It's all the other "stuff" we choose to pile on our plates that causes us to be tired and fall short.

News flash: Whatever is on your plate is there because you said yes to it. When we assume someone else's assignment, the extra stress and required energy to complete it ends up consuming us. Even stars in the sky have an expiration date. They may have a long life to live, but they will eventually burn out.

King David shared with us in Psalm 57:2, (JUB) "I will cry unto God most high, unto God who performs all things for me." What I hear David saying in this verse is no matter what obstacles or adversities came his way, he was going to continue to trust God and stand firm on the promise God made over his life. The question is, do we really believe what King David is telling us? If so, then we should never worry about our own lives and definitely not lose any sleep over anyone else's life. This is because God has full authority over everything that happens to us. God is above any job, obstacle, relationship, or sickness, and He is working through any addiction, dilemma, problem, or struggle we have so that we can fulfill His purpose. We all make the mistake of trying to fulfill God's purpose for someone else's life. However, just because you share the same last name with someone, doesn't mean you were called to help them fulfill *their* purpose in life.

I realize making hard choices on the "field of life" can, at times, be tough, but don't confuse sacrifice with stupidity. You should not let the assignments of others distract you from what God has already told you to do. Throughout my career in the NFL, I gained the reputation of being a very smart player who was never out of position. I was consistent, dependable, and reliable. I played at a very high level, and I always did my job first. I often saw my teammates and other players around the league get themselves in trouble by trying to do someone else's job. Or worse yet, trying to do too much. Doing too much in the world of sports will eventually get you exposed and your team defeated. This same principle holds true in the "game" of life. If we don't decide what's important to us and make it clear to those around us, we'll always find ourselves doing only what is important to others.

## Choosing Your Assignment

I often wonder who to help and who not to help. This is a struggle for all of us, simply because no one person has the resources or time to help everyone. Even for those who are blessed and fortunate enough to have an abundance of resources, they don't have the power to change the number of hours in a day or control when their clock stops. In fact, time is the only thing that we all have in common. Because we all have limitations, no one ever has it all.

What makes me give money to one guy on the corner and ignore the guy on the next corner? At times, this question weighs heavy on my heart, because I truly enjoy blessing others and genuinely want to help people. But I don't want to handicap them or get in the way of God's work in their lives. Because we desire to help others, particularly our families and those we love, we need to establish solid guidelines to address needs and requests. And hopefully, this will help us make wise choices, because the more successful you are, the more demands there will be on your time and money. My favorite rapper of all time, the Notorious B.I.G., said it best: "Mo Money, Mo Problems." Trust me, he was not just rapping or saying that because it sounded good.

Over many years of personally being burned and making bad choices, here's what's helped me make better decisions when attempting to decipher if something is my true assignment versus if I'm just assuming something is my assignment. I ask myself several questions before I engage in something I'm unsure about:

- Is what I am being asked to do producing a vision?
- Am I fully equipped and prepared to take on what's being asked of me?
- Am I deeply passionate about it?
- Is my heart 100 percent in it? If not, my head won't stay focused on it long enough to see it through.
- Is this something I must do, or is it something someone wants me to do?
- Has God truly called me for this assignment?
- Am I making assumptions about this person based on an experience with someone else?
- Who benefits?
- Should I bless them, or should I continue to pray for them?

Remembering my assignment, avoiding the temptation of

making emotional decisions, separating what I know to be true from what someone is projecting to be true, and not living by assumptions, have all played a major part in helping me mature in this area of my life. When I reach the end of my life and have no more time-outs, and all the television commercials have aired, and I'm all out of red challenge flags, and there's no more time on my clock, I believe I'll be judged based on how well I completed the assignments God specifically gave me. Some aspects of my assignments are very clear: Love God, love and nurture my wife and children, honor my parents, and love others like Jesus loves us. But some aspects of life's purpose can seem a little foggy, and this is where assumptions can get in the way of wisdom. True assignments from God are always so much bigger than ourselves and are always a blessing to others.

We often *assume* we're supposed to automatically help someone because of many logical-sounding reasons, like: *We've been friends forever,* or *he's my cousin,* or *because mom asked me to,* or *because I'm in a better situation than they're in,* or *that's what family is for.* When we immediately assume, we don't necessarily stop to consider if the opportunity is fulfilling our assignment, or if it's a dressed-up assumption in the form of a distraction, mixed with its ugly cousin called emotions.

Let me explain a bit more. By distraction, I don't mean helping people is necessarily a mistake. But, when mixing relationships and financial help, it doesn't take much to dominate a person's calendar and emotional life or to lead them off track.

So, the real question is: What's the true cost of not following the assignment God gave you? I'm not sure about you, but I don't have forty years of my life to spare wandering around lost in the woods.

What if we become so distracted and deplete our emotional and financial resources that we miss out on the opportunities to connect with the people we're assigned to and uniquely gifted to help? This would result in many of us dying with our seeds in our pockets and the other half of us not reaching our full potential in life.

## Assumptions Work Both Ways

Bank of America doesn't stay open twenty-four hours a day, so why is it that some people expect others to dispense cash at any time of day, seven days a week, 365 days out of the year? I know you'll quickly say that ATMs were created for this very reason. And I couldn't agree more. But for this very same reason, most banks will put a limit on how much you can withdraw from the ATM at any given time. God said He would supply all our needs, not all our wants. So, if God Almighty isn't signing an unlimited contract, then, why are we? Why do we feel like we must supply all our loved ones' needs and their wants? God has already promised to take care of their needs, so, it's time for us to reclaim our lives and give others back the responsibility for their own lives.

We sometimes assume our help is necessary for every situation, and that can be an unhealthy mind-set. We must realize a situation can go from bad to worse when we believe we should always help. We all, in some way or another, have been prewired with our own assumptions about certain things in life, and we don't even realize it. One of my biggest assumptions in life was thinking money could fix my family. Growing up, I thought the scarcity, or lack of money, was our biggest problem.

When I was first drafted, and when I signed my second deal with the Tennessee Titans, I assumed if I paid off everyone in my immediate family's bills, debts, loans, and cars and gifted them with some of the things they'd always wished for, we'd be a happy family again. I assumed they would then be able to save money and live without the normal stresses of life. That is, if they continued to work their jobs and not change their lifestyle habits. Most people find themselves getting into trouble because of what they start doing, but even more of us find ourselves in trouble because of what we stop doing. Just because someone pays off your bills doesn't mean you have money to blow.

Fix your facial expression, please. I know what you're thinking: *The money I was paying on my house, car, and student loans, can now all go in my pocket.* Great analysis! If you're smart and you're seriously trying to get your own financial independence, you'd continue to live like you were before your bills were paid off and put that money in the bank. House payments, car payments, student loans, and debt are most people's biggest bills or struggles. With those major bills eliminated, I thought I was setting my family up to succeed, but in reality, I was failing them. Badly! I caught, cleaned, and cooked all the fish for them, but I never once taught them how to catch a fish on their own. A great friend of mine once told me, "If your problem can be solved by simply writing a check, then what you had was an expense, not a problem."

This expression also comes to mind: "Fool me once, shame on you. Fool me twice, shame on me." I've been fooled a dozen times by some people. Don't even ask me what that level of shame and disappointment feels like. I look back over my life now, and I just have to laugh to keep from crying or getting angry. I wish I could go back to those moments and change things. Instead of giving money, I would offer some good advice. I would advise them to quit their day jobs and pursue an acting career, because they sure made a believer out of me. Through all my shame, I've desperately searched for the good and valuable lessons. Today, I can boldly say these lessons have helped me develop a resolve to focus on my God-given purpose.

When the people you care about begin to assume you'll not only take care of them in an emergency but also become their everyday provider, no one is helped. Unless you've committed to providing for someone or signed a lifetime contract to take care of them, any assumption on their part is unhealthy. In other words, stop the madness before it escalates to the next level. And believe me, if you don't like the current dynamics of the relationship, it will only get worse if you don't stick to your assignment and establish boundaries.

Yes, some stuff may hit the fan. But you can always get a new fan. Or use a stronger air freshener. Within a relationship, there will never be an authentic appreciation if there is an underlying expectation. The day we learn to shift our focus from expectation to appreciation, is the day our lives will change.

## Emotions Versus Assignments

Bishop Walker always says, "Feeling and being in the presence of the Lord is a spiritual encounter, not a fleshly experience." In other words, we don't serve God based on our feelings. Proverbs 19:21 says, "There are many devices in a man's heart; nevertheless the counsel of the Lord, that shall stand." I suppose my translation would be something like, "Emotions come and go. Follow God's Word, and the assignment in your heart, even when it's not easy. Especially when it's not easy. Focus on His promise and not on the pain you are feeling—personally or for someone else."

One way to identify between assignment and assumption is to stop and evaluate. Ask yourself: *Is this a situation I'm called to be involved in, or am I operating out of someone's wrong expectation?* We must have conviction in our decisions to be truly successful. And let's face it, we all are blessed when we see someone living by Godly convictions—even when their decisions don't please everyone. There's no amount of money that can ever refill your emotional bank account after being manipulated by someone close to you. And there's no worldly reward that compares to the thrill of living out your assignment.

## A Clear Conscience

Some people give to their church and other charities from wrong motivations. The Bible is clear that we should not give "grudgingly." We're also instructed to not give while we have unforgiveness or anger toward someone. So why don't we apply these same standards when helping family and friends?

Anger, unforgiveness, and resentment are warning signs that we're operating out of assumptions and veering from our assignments. Just think about that for a minute. Even God doesn't want His own money back from us if we aren't being cheerful about it. So, we have to understand that God has not blessed or condoned any transaction between you and someone else who's willing to accept a gift from you when you aren't seeing eye to eye. Helping in a situation like this may be a good thing, but it's definitely not a God thing.

## Your Number One Job

Your number one job in life is to follow your purpose. If you don't know where you're going, you'll follow anyone. Platinum recording artist J. Cole in his single titled "Love Yourz" express-es how it's such a positive thing for us to look back over our lives and celebrate how far we've come, only to be heartbroken once we realize the entire time we've been going the wrong way.

When you do realize where you're headed in life, you'll soon discover you won't be able to please everyone. There is an old, but true, saying: "If you try to please everyone, you end up pleasing no one." There's also a more modern version: "Trying to please everyone is impossible, but pissing everyone off is a piece of cake."

Why do you think Proverbs 22:26-27 warns against "help-ing" someone by co-signing a loan or becoming responsible for their debt? As a general practice, don't allow family members or friends to put things in your name that you don't own. If they need a name to put their possessions in, tell them to put their house or car in Jesus' name. Trust me on this one! Becoming responsible for someone else's debt never ends well, and both parties will eventually be hurt.

I firmly believe that we all should take personal owner-ship for the outcome of our lives. This means caring only for those we're assigned to help. In the Bible, when Jesus went to the graveyard where Lazarus was buried to wake him from the dead, Jesus specifically called Lazarus' name. If He would have just told the dead to rise, every person buried would've risen from their grave! But, Jesus didn't heal every person He walked by. I don't pretend to understand why, but I do know He completed His assignment.

The most important dates of our lives are our birth dates and the date we realize why we were born. When we finally commit to our purpose in life, our lives gain momentum, and we become clear on what God expects from us. We need to be in the business of pleasing Him, not pleasing people. When we wholeheartedly come to terms with that, the rest of the people will humbly fall back and stay in their lanes. It's amazing how there are never any accidents (or heavy traffic on the road) when everyone stays in their own lane.

Do me a favor. Take out a sheet a paper and write down all your responsibilities. Think of these as your job description, so to speak. After doing this, ask yourself: "Would you fire yourself?" If the answer to this question is yes, you must remind yourself that you're only responsible for doing what you wrote down. If you truly believe this, you then have the power to change or rewrite the requirements to what you want to be held responsible for. You're the one who's ultimately in charge of your life. This will help you see the difference between what you *need* to do versus what others *want* you to do.

Your number one job in life is to follow your purpose. So, let me ask you again: If it's not a part of your assignment, why is it on your calendar? Why is it in your checkbook? Why is it keeping you up at night?

# TURNOVERS

- When we make it our jobs to provide for all our loved ones' needs and wants, we handicap them for life. This is because the "help" we provide makes it hard for them to readjust and become self-motivated.
- We make the mistake of living by assumptions, which leads to us making emotional decisions.
- We automatically think it's our responsibility to save everybody and make it our mission to help them fulfill their purpose in life.

# TAKEAWAYS

- Don't schedule or plan to do something that's not important enough to make it on your calendar.
- Our most important or valuable resource is not our money—it's our time. We all have the same 24 hours in a day, but no one knows how much time they have left. Stop letting others waste your time. As Bishop T.D. Jakes says, "I would rather a person waste any and everything I have, rather than waste my time."
- It's our responsibility to love our loved ones, not save them.

# Chapter 7

# GIFT VERSUS CURSE

Matthew 19:24 teaches us, "It is easier for a camel to walk through the eye of a needle, than for a rich man to enter the kingdom of God." My grandfather shared this gut-wrenching verse with me one day while he and I were sitting on the front porch relaxing, after one of my early morning workouts, a few days after I was drafted by the Pittsburgh Steelers. As he began to walk back inside the house to refill his glass jar with ice, after patiently waiting for all the ice to melt to water before he would even take a sip, he calmly said, "I'd hate to be you, son . . ."

Wealth solves a lot of problems, and it creates a lot of new ones, too. With that said, most people would still much rather be wealthy than not. Or, I should probably say most people want the money and the fame, but they don't want the problems and responsibilities that come along with them. My Uncle Gully, one of my dad's older brothers, once told a friend of mine at the barbershop one Saturday morning, "Everybody wants to be like Chris, but I would much rather be Rodney, Chris's brother. He gets everything Chris gets, but he doesn't have to work out, get hit, worry about some young boy trying to take his job every year, or stress himself out trying to please his family all the time."

Being in the position or situation where you can change the financial landscape for your family, close friends, and generations to come and still afford to make a huge impact in the world, is an amazing gift and responsibility. A great friend, former Tennessee Titans teammate, Florida State University (FSU) alumni, a brother of mine, and just a brilliant human being, Myron Rolle, shared with me "that the responsibility is so great, because when your future relatives look back at their family history, they will look at you and say this is the point where the trajectory of our family went from being flat to an exponential increase quickly. The curve on the graph has been, is, and will be, dictated by you."

It's truly a blessing to be able to provide things we dreamed of as children to our loved ones, but without wise boundaries, the gift can quickly turn into a curse. Resentment is like a person drinking poison then hoping for their enemy to die. The very people whom, at one point in our lives, we would've been willing to run through a wall for and give our last to, have now become the very people we resent and despise. On the flip side, those same people, at one point in time, before all the success and money came, probably would've considered doing the same for us. It's amazing how a family can be so happy being poor but fall apart when it becomes rich. The struggle is very real. I know you are reading this and probably thinking to yourself, "Wait a minute; that doesn't make any sense." Welcome to my world. Those are the same perplexing thoughts and feelings I have continuously beat myself up with over the past fifteen plus years.

In Luke 12:48, Jesus said, "To whom much is given, much more is required." In short, the more blessings we're entrusted with, the higher the level of responsibility and accountability we're held to. It's a test, plain and simple. As they say, "No test, no testimony." And, as with any test, we can pass or fail. As with any opportunity, we can either fall back or step up to the challenge. That's the difference between a gift and a curse—how we handle what has been given to us.

Sure, the pressure can become overwhelming. Just the thought alone, right now, is draining me of all my energy and making me super-stressed. As I said earlier, relationships can get complicated. Especially when it comes to family, close friends, and money. That's why I believe all relationships, blood-related or not, must be built, or centered around, a friendship first. This way, the foundation of the relationship is deeply rooted, and the unconditional bond is strong enough to weather any storm. At the end of the day, any relationship, friendship, partnership, or fellowship that doesn't have Jesus at the center of it will become a hardship.

When the phone rings and everything in your body cringes,

please know that's not a normal feeling or reaction when you receive a phone call. But for me, it's become my life. Determining whether to answer the phone, at times, has started to become a more serious thought for me than deciding to send my children to private or public school. Seriously, I mean you must look at both as an investment. One is short-term; whereas, the other is long-term. However, only one is likely to be a true return on your investment. Please, take note of the subliminal message behind what I just said.

Unfortunately, I have grown hesitant to answer the phone, because I automatically assume it's probably another request for financial help or because something bad has happened. This can become so overwhelming at times, it may force you to continuously change your phone number, due to the consistent "emergency" calls you receive from your family and friends, or because you were forced to give your number out to avoid appearing rude to someone. Things can get so bad, you may have to buy an entirely separate phone or constantly screen all your calls.

I'm not proud to say this, but it's the truth. I've been known to encourage a person with whom I've just exchanged my contact information with to call me right on the spot, while I'm still standing there in front of them. Not so much for them to make sure they've stored my number correctly in their phone. It's more for me to lock their number in my phone. So, whenever they decide to cold-call me, their name will pop up on my screen, and I won't blindly answer. I know I'm not the only one who does this. It's sad, but true. Please, forgive me.

Over the years, I've found that it's been easier for me to say "no" when I've chosen not to open my spirit and allow myself to be exposed to the depressing stories people want to unload. People have no problem using you as their emotional dumpster. This doesn't apply to everyone, so don't think I'm heartless or insensitive. But, I will say, it's becoming harder and harder to separate the real from the fake.

We can't blame others for all our problems. Money creates opportunities and exposes weaknesses in our character as well. Bottom line: Money not only changes things—it also changes people. There's an old saying: "Money allows people to be a bigger version of what they already are." According to the National Endowment for Financial Education, about 70 percent of lottery winners, and those receiving large amounts of money, will go bankrupt a few years after cashing in on their winnings.[2]

## The True Nature of Blessing

The wealthiest person who has ever lived experienced both the gifts and the curses of riches. That's why his inspired proverb is so interesting. King Solomon lived in abundance and excess. Proverbs 10:22 shares how he finally made sense of his wealth: "The blessings of the Lord makes one rich, and He adds no

---

2. http://www.cleveland.com/business/index.ssf/2016/01/why_do_70_percent_of_lottery_w.html

sorrow with it." This scripture comes to life when the gift of wealth is placed in the hands of a mature person, one who understands the kingdom, including the principles, purposes, and proper stewardship of it. The curse comes when the gift of wealth is placed in the hands of someone who lives outside of God's will and then uses their wealth for selfish reasons. I've grown to understand there are really only three things we can do with our money: save, give, or invest it. Nevertheless, our egocentric and self-serving mind-sets have created a fourth use for money: squandering it.

God's blessings will enrich us. Period. This fact is crucial to understanding and handling wealth. The "sorrows" we might experience because of our success and wealth don't come from God. If that is true, then where do the hassles and heartaches come from? The answer isn't far. We only need to look in the mirror to find out.

## Curses

One of the curses of becoming financially affluent is other people become dependent upon you, seeing you as their financial savior and expecting you to rescue them from all types of situations. There is no worse feeling than having the means to do whatever you want to do in life but being reluctant to do so, because you worry about not having enough to sustain your own lifestyle and the lifestyle of your loved ones.

My friend Myron went on to express his views as it relates to the curse of being the gifted or chosen one in the family. He says, "The curse is that you no longer are just living for yourself. Your every move and action are micro-managed and micro-analyzed by everyone, always. Your life is no longer your own; it belongs to the same people who have benefited from that exponential growth on that curve in which you made happen."

The burden of being responsible for your loved ones is, and always will be, an enormous amount of pressure. The pressure of always keeping your edge and never being able to relax and enjoy the fruits of your labor is intense, because you're responsible for so many other people. You end up never being able to take off your game face or let down your guard, because it's so difficult to trust people. Not being allowed to say or show you're hurting and desire emotional assistance without being considered weak can also take its toll. As can being forced to stay silent and keep all your authentic emotions bottled up due to being misunderstood and being held to a different standard just because you aren't struggling financially.

Constant pressure like this can cause a young person to age rather quickly. The stress and tension can also cause serious physical and mental health issues. The sad part is, most of the people you're providing for are grown adults who have no jobs and have already enjoyed living their lives however they damn-well pleased. The only thing that has changed is now they're trying to dictate and monitor your every move.

Your gift can easily become strangled, or your candle blown out, by always having to think for others or by living one or two, or even three, steps ahead, planning and preparing for someone else's poor decisions. Celso Cukierkorn shares that, "Poverty is a result of poor choices, not of poor luck." The curse of always being the dependable, disciplined, and responsible one, while everyone else lives in a reckless, irresponsible, and carefree manner in pursuit of finding their best life, gets old fast.

Dealing with the uncertainties of knowing when to help someone in need and knowing when not to, can make a person's hair turn gray or completely disappear overnight. I'm not blaming anyone for my bald head and salt-and-pepper beard, but I'm sure not pardoning anyone either. The guilt of having the ability to help someone in need and choosing not to, only to later deal with heavy doses of regret is an awful feeling. It can make a person question God for even giving them the gift. I have caught myself several times asking, "God, why me?" The minute I finish questioning God, I often hear a small, distinct voice saying, "Because I can trust you and you can handle it!"

## Grace and Gump

On January 4, 2000, my Florida State Seminoles team defeated the Virginia Tech Hokies 46-29 to clinch the 1999 BCS National-al Championship. I was a part of three different teams in the NFL that won more than thirteen games in one season: The 2004

Steelers went 15-1, the 2008 Titans went 13-3, and the 2012 Falcons went 13-3. How ironic is that? The number four has always been my favorite number growing up, and God always seems to do extraordinary things in my life every four years.

As I mentioned earlier, I had the honor of being part of the team with Jerome Bettis, who played and won the Super Bowl in his hometown in the final game of his career. As a Pittsburgh Steeler, our team won the organization's fifth Super Bowl: "One for the Thumb." We were the first team in NFL playoff history to win the Super Bowl as the sixth seed, and we were the first team in NFL history to win three roads games leading up to the Super Bowl.

As a thirteen-year-old high school freshman, I started on my school's varsity football team, playing alongside my older brother, Rodney, in his senior season. At the time of my graduation, I held the state record for starting fifty-five consecutive games. Remarkably, I started on offense and defense my junior and senior seasons. And, in middle school, my eighth-grade football team went undefeated and unscored-upon the entire season.

At FSU, I played on the first and only undefeated team under Coach Bobby Bowden. We were the first team in college football history to be ranked number one in the country from the start of the season to the end. And we were the first team to win the BCS National Championship.

I had the honor of playing under legendary coaches such as Bill Cowher, Bobby Bowden, and Dick LeBeau, a Pro Football Hall of Fame coach and player. I had the privilege to play alongside legendary teammates in both college and the NFL. Some of my Florida State teammates included: 2000 Heisman Trophy Award winner Chris Weinke, Peter Warrick, 2000 Lombardi Award winner and roommate Jamal Reynolds, two-time Lou Groza Award winner Sebastian Janikowski, Anquan Boldin, Corey Simon, Derrick Gibson, Travis Minor, Javon Walker, Darnell Dockett, Greg Jones, and many more. My professional teammates included: Hall of Famer Jerome Bettis, Hines Ward, Troy Polamalu, James Harrison, Alan Faneca, Plaxico Burress, Casey Hampton, James Farrior, Joey Porter, Kevin Mawae, Chris Johnson, Cortland Finnegan, Michael Griffin, Keith Bulluck, Jevon Kearse, Vince Young, Adam "Pacman" Jones, Len-Dale White, Albert Haynesworth, Alge Crumpler, Kyle Vanden Bosch, Randy Moss, Brent Grimes, Asante Samuel, Julio Jones, Tony Gonzalez, Roddy White, Matt Ryan, Ben Roethlisberger, Kordell Stewart, Antwaan Randle El, Duce Staley, and many others. A few of whom, in my opinion, will also one day become Hall of Famers.

I was the first native from my hometown of Rock Hill, South Carolina, to win a Super Bowl. I was also the first to be selected to the Pro Bowl, the first to be named a USA Today High School All-American, the first to be rated the number-one player in the state, and the first player to be named "Mr. Football" for the state of South Carolina. After winning the National Championship in 1999, I met President Clinton. And after winning the Super Bowl in 2005, I met President Bush.

After many years of failing to make it, or being flat out snubbed by the Pro Bowl, I was fortunate enough to be selected to play in the last Pro Bowl in Hawaii under the traditional NFL format. I don't share these stories to boast or brag about my life and successes. I share them to give you insight on how blessed I have been to be at the right place at the right time. And how grateful and humbled I am by God choosing to use me in this way. The better you know me, the more my story sounds like the film character Forrest Gump. It all comes down to grace and persistence. What I appreciate most about Forrest is that he took it all in stride and didn't let success go to his head.

## Star in Your Role

With social media, everyone knows your next move—what you're doing and when. As a result, everyone has their own two cents to donate to your timeline. When you post your plans, you have openly welcomed the world's opinion. It's almost like the minute you become famous or reach a certain status, you forever forfeit your privacy and experience a loss of ownership for your own life. A lot of this falls on our own shoulders as celebrities, athletes, and entertainers. To stay relevant, or remain in the spotlight, such celebrities expose their lives to the world to give their fans a closer look into their everyday lifestyles, which, in turn, only creates more criticism, drama, and judgment. All for what cost? Your safety? Your sanity? Just to get more votes to make an All-Star game? To create a large following or to seal a lucrative endorsement from some private company? Picture that. You give up your privacy and safety for a check, while companies hide behind your face and brand and collect more money than they're willing to pay you.

For a lot of really famous people, their fame really becomes their curse—like the Michael Jacksons and Princes of the world. Being able to go to a grocery store, pump gas, or walk through the airport alone becomes forbidden for them. The normalcy of everyday life is no longer an option. Think about Tiger Woods' amazing fall from glory. Or Ervin "Magic" Johnson's announcement to the world about contracting the HIV virus. And let's not forget the national spectacle of the O. J. Simpson trial. I have to wonder, who made it okay for the lives of the rich and famous to be an open book for the world's entertainment, all because they are well-known or have a high net worth? Why is their business the world's business? Here's a free piece of advice for you: If you ever have the choice on whether to become rich or famous, always choose rich.

Today, it doesn't take much to be locally "famous," and with fame, no matter the platform or the number of followers, comes pressure and danger. Everything you do is publicized and scrutinized. Anyone can Google how much money you make and find out where you live when you're considered a celebrity or reach a certain level of success. You can even Google an athlete's game schedule or find out the tour dates of a hot new entertainer who may be coming to your city. Pictures of your spouse and kids can be found on the internet, along with what kind of vehicle you drive and where you frequently hang out. To me, it all sounds like an open invitation for someone to swing by and check on your house while you're on vacation to help jump-start your moving process or encourage someone to follow you home and do harm to you and your family. This type of behavior can become frightening, especially for your family and loved ones.

To add salt to the wound, the public has the nerve to form a negative opinion about celebrities who carry guns and are surrounded by bodyguards and entourages to help them feel safe. The second something happens, it's so easy for the public to loudly voice their thoughts about what they think occurred or what they feel the consequences should be. I get so angry and frustrated hearing people say, "It does not take all that security and crowd of people to feel safe," or "They are stupid for being around that type of stuff after becoming so successful." I find these types of remarks both mind-boggling and extremely disturbing.

Some people, I call them "serial fans," often know the ins and outs of an athlete's contract better than the athlete. Whose idea was it to make a person's specific contract, net worth, or personal address public information? I think this transparency comes at a great cost to the celebrity. Whether they want it or not, their lives become the world's reality show, but for them, it's far from a game. It's peoples' real lives we're talking about here. Fantasy football is just that—a fantasy. But, this isn't a movie or pretend game for us. There are no stuntmen, body doubles, or fictitious characters. We are real people with real feelings just like everyone else in the world.

## Gifts

So, how do we keep a gift a gift and not let it become a curse in our lives? Embracing the gift and resisting the curse takes discipline and strength. It goes back to the still, small voice inside of you—the voice of God's Spirit—and learning to be guided by that voice. One of the best ways to hear that voice more clearly is to stop what you're doing and listen. The words "silent" and "listen" both share the same letters. The reason some of us can't listen is because we won't be silent. To hear the whisper of God, we must turn down the volume of the world. Then, we must simply ask Him what we want to know and what we need to know. Albert Einstein once said, "I want to know God's thoughts—the rest are mere details."

Staying humble and grounded is critical, and this is where healthy family relationships can be a real gift. We all need open, honest communication with family, because they are the people who can help keep us grounded.

If you lose close bonds with the people you love, that's when your guard is down, which makes you more vulnerable and could even cause you to allow outsiders and strangers into your camp. Most of the newcomers who enter your circle when the celebrity status has already been achieved and the money has already been made will only be "yes men." These people have one job—and that's to say "yes" to whatever you say. Unfortunately, hearing "yes" all the time will make any person start to believe their stuff does not stink and cause them to fall in the danger zone of being worshipped. This is why we'll find ourselves asking, "Who are his parents and where are his real friends?" when watching someone act foolishly on television. Only God is to be worshipped.

Bishop Walker always reminds the athletic community of his church, "If we allow ourselves to be worshipped by others, we will have a hard time learning to worship God, which will eventually lead to our demise." The best thing you can do is to stay grounded is to find trustworthy friends who have your best interest at heart. I've tried my best to keep the same group of people around me, my longtime friends and family. My best friend and I actually talk every day. And I hang out with my brother and sister often. My cousins and I, along with everyone else I just mentioned, spend a lot of time together reminiscing about the good old days and all the fun times we had growing up together. Other than that, I am spending time with my immediate family—Linda and the kids.

When it comes to friends, the gift of friendships can only

thrive when there are no unrealistic expectations of each other. Friendships, or any healthy relationships for that matter, are designed to be reciprocal. Each partner should make it their responsibility to pour into the other partner. In Proverbs 27:17, the Bible says, "As iron sharpens iron, so a friend sharpens a friend."

In the end, we're responsible for taking care of the riches and the relationships God blesses us with. We can't blame friends, family, or Facebook for our sorrows. Instead, we must look to the rewards of investing in our legacy.

## TURNOVERS

- When we initially give everyone we meet, including our own family members, an 850 FICO score, we put ourselves at risk. Start them off at zero and make them build up their "credit."
- When we make the mistake of cutting ties with our real family members and true friends to surround ourselves with "yes" men who only tell us what we want to hear, we make ourselves vulnerable to being preyed upon by those who may not have our best interests at heart.
- When we fall victim to the lure of adoration and acceptance, and it becomes difficult to imagine living without being famous, we allow people to start worshiping us.

## TAKEAWAYS

- All relationships, including those with relatives, should be built on a foundation of friendship. This way the relationship will have a healthy amount of give-and-take. You can tell who's a true friend when both of you don't need anything from each other.
- Guard your heart and mind at all times. Don't be everyone's emotional dumpster: Be careful what you allow people to drop into your spirit.
- "Be humble," like Kendrick Lamar says. Learn how to be blessed but not boisterous.

# Chapter 8

# PRIVATE PAIN VERSUS PUBLIC PRAISE

There's an old church fable about a man complaining to Jesus about how heavy and difficult it was to carry His cross. He asked Jesus if he could exchange the cross for a much smaller one, or at least trade with someone to help lighten his load. The man went on to express to Jesus how he saw other people carrying crosses that were much easier to handle and how effortless they made it look.

Jesus decided to make a deal with the man. He led the man into a room full of crosses made of all different shapes and sizes. Some were big. Whereas, others were small, but pointy and awkwardly shaped. The only instruction Jesus gave the man was once he put down his cross, he could choose from any of the crosses in the room. But after making his choice on his new cross, he could never complain or exchange his cross again.

The man started his search for a new cross, walking around

the room, closely examining every cross he passed. To his sur-prise, every cross he looked at had something he complained about or did not like. After hours of looking, he finally found a cross he thought would be perfect for him.

The man shouted out to Jesus, "Here it is Lord. I've finally found the perfect cross for me." Jesus asked the man "Are you certain on your decision?" The man answered, "I'm sure." Jesus then replied, "My child, that is the very same cross you were carrying when you came in to see me."

The moral of the story is we all have a cross to bear and God has equipped and empowered us with everything we need to carry the cross He has given us. We'll all be faced with trials and tribulations and deal with our own unique struggles in life. No one is immune to that. We just have to wait until it's our turn. As stated in Job 14:1, "Man that is born of a woman is of a few days and full of trouble."

## I Wish I Had Their Life

At times, have you felt like someone else was living a better life than the one you were living? It's hard to focus on and feel envi-ous about the life and gifts God has blessed someone else with, when we are truly maximizing all the gifts He has given us. To wish you had another person's life is like saying God made a mistake with the life He has given you. If you have, don't feel bad or beat yourself up about it. We've all been there before. And since I'm soliciting your undivided attention and your time in reading my book, I'll be completely open with you. I've been guilty of this—in two completely different scenarios.

The first time I experience this was when I was growing up, watching pro athletes, celebrities, and entertainers. I wanted their same lifestyle, at least the one glamorously portrayed to us on television. The money, the cars, the clothes, the houses, the jewelry, the fame, the beautiful women—I wanted it all.

The second time I experienced this came years after my successful NFL career. When my life, at times, became so chaotic, I'd sometimes look at those with "simpler" lives and think, *I wish I had their life*. Too many unknowns and not enough guarantees come along with any professional career. So, you can only imagine the level of uncertainty you might feel when you enter into the world of professional sports. In fact, uncertainty is the only thing that's certain.

From the outside looking in, people would probably think I didn't have any problems. They probably thought everything was perfect and always had been in Chris Hope's world. Most people would probably consider me to be privileged. They may even have thought: *Chris comes from a two-parent home with both parents working good paying jobs. He has two older siblings that both were good athletes, and they both graduated from college. He was always the talk of the town and loved by everyone that knew him. Chris Hope has no struggles, pains, worries, or anything to cry about. Everything has always come so easy for him.*

But in reality, that's far from the truth. I'm no different than you. The amount of stress and pressure of living up to the high expectations I set for myself, as well as those set by everyone watching and waiting for me to fail, made me feel like I had the weight of the world on my shoulders. I've had to work hard for, and earn, everything I've achieved. Nothing has been given to me. I have everyday life issues just like everyone else. To be honest, I probably deal with more problems in most cases.

## Duck in a Pond

A few years ago, I watched a documentary on NBA Hall of Famer and perennial All-Star Allen Iverson's life. Being a few years older than I am, I obviously was a big fan and follower of his career. But ESPN and every other news outlet that allowed the fans to get a closer glimpse of his life behind the scenes, while he still played in the NBA, painted only the picture they wanted us to see, whether good or bad. This documentary was filmed many years after he hung up his sneakers. It exposed the good, the bad, and the ugly of his childhood and his life while in the NBA. One part, in particular, stood out to me, and it really impacted my life.

An older gentleman from the neighborhood where Iverson grew up in was interviewed and was asked to describe, in his own words, what he thought about the life of Allen Iverson. The seasoned gentleman said, "Bubba Chuck's life was like that of a duck swimming in a pond. On the surface, it looked like he was just floating along effortlessly. But underneath the surface, he was kicking like hell, fighting for his life, trying to stay afloat." The irony and imagery in that saying hit home with me on so many different levels. It left me speechless. That phrase is the modern-day slogan for, "Fake it till you make it."

So many of us have perfected putting on our game faces, that it's impossible to call our own bluffs. We've mastered the art of driving around town on empty. The world is filled with imperfect people, but we still try our best to walk around like everything is perfect, and we have no problems. I get it. It's very difficult to express to those who are depending on us to survive that we're on "E," be it spiritually, physically, emotionally, and even financially.

When our lives are running on empty, it's very important for us to realize where our help comes from. In doing so, we'll come to terms with trusting God to do what we cannot do. If not, we will be more prone to turn to the world to find meaning through drugs, alcohol, sex, or gambling. Instead, we must learn to trust God even when we can't trace Him. Even when things don't pan out the way we planned. When we give our weaknesses to God, in return, He will give us His strength. We must be brave enough to go as far as we can see, to be able to see how far we can go. God will take care of the things we can't, while we focus on taking care of ourselves. In the process, we need to eliminate our superhero attitudes and stop trying to do what God has already done. Only one person can save the world, and last I checked that was still God's job.

One of the main reasons I wrote this book was to give you

a cheat sheet. I wanted to spare you from any unnecessary pain and to give you a wise and wide perspective on success. Paradoxically, some of the most "successful" people are often the most "unsuccessful" in what really matters the most in life: family, memories, and experiences. All-Pro and three-time Defensive MVP of the NFL J. J. Watts said, "Success isn't owned. It's leased, and rent is due every day."

Sure, I have a wonderful, beautiful wife and terrific, healthy kids. Financially, life is not bad at all. But few people realize the physical and emotional pain I carry on the inside. Since I played the game of football from the age of seven and didn't stop until I was in my mid-thirties, the physical pain can be, at times, overwhelming, but that is somewhat expected. Even still, some people think we are gladiators, and we don't know what pain really is. At one time, I may have agreed with them, but now I know better.

During one off-season, I had several discs in my neck protruding outward, threatening to damage my spine. As a result, I had my C3 and C4 vertebrae surgically fused together. As of late, my entire neck has naturally fused together on its own, trying to protect itself. I have extremely limited mobility in my neck, which causes a lot of daily aches and pains. I also have headaches that are just as consistent as a person who blinks their eyes. Sleep at night is few and far and between. I experience weakness and nerve issues in my right arm that extend all the way down into my right hand that will probably follow me to the grave. In fact, my neck injury prompted me to retire. Most people don't know how much my left forearm aches. When I walk, my knees sound off like shotguns being fired. In addition, my ankles crack on every stride, both of my shoulders constantly throb, my lower back shouts at me, and my neck pain travels freely around my body like it has an unlimited hall pass.

Emotionally, I've been an even bigger prisoner to pain. At the time, very few people knew that Linda and I had a horrible breakup the first time we got engaged or that she packed up all her stuff and went back to Miami while I was playing in an away game against the New York Jets. In all my years of living, I've never experienced walking inside a house that felt so cold, empty, and spiritless. After she left Tennessee, we didn't talk to each other for almost nine months. And very few people knew that my parents went through a divorce after being married for nearly thirty years. Or that there were drugs and domestic violence in the Hope house when I was growing up. To be honest, I feel like the drugs packed their bags first and were waiting on the front porch for us when we arrived to start moving our new furniture into the bigger house.

And no one knew I had two defensive coordinators, in back-to-back seasons, take my love for the game of football away from me. I'm not a violent person, but it was so bad that if I could've gotten away with it, and not jeopardized my job and reputation, hitting those two coaches would've probably been two of the hardest hits of my career. I still struggle with feelings of anger toward those two men to this day.

And no one knew, including myself, that I was going through a deep depression, which dates all the way back to my senior year in college. I would go months at a time without talking to my parents and other important family members. I'm presently still struggling with this. I learned from a young age how to wear my "game face" and mask any pain I was going through. During those back-to-back dark seasons, I would wake up at 5:15 a.m. and be at the facility at 6:00 a.m. to work out, study film, or receive treatment. Anything to get out of my lonely house was a respite, but I truly hated going to the facility to see the coaches I despised. For the first time in my life, football wasn't even my safe haven. Regardless of how bad I felt, being around the game and my teammates was better than being home. I would stay after practice and watch film with my defensive back coach, Marcus Roberston, until 10:00 or 11:00 at night. I was getting zero hours of sleep, but no one could tell. As a matter fact, no one even asked. I was a programmed professional. A highly-functional zombie.

## What Does Public Praise Look Like?

This is the fun part. Why everyone, including other celebrities, wants to be an athlete. Where should I begin? Public praise includes VIP treatment at restaurants, the airport, and all the nightclubs—even at the hospital or the doctors' and dentists' offices. You also get backstage passes, front-row seats at concerts, floor seats at NBA games, the hookup on merchandise (clothes and shoes), and special rates and preferential treatment at banks. If you're really big time, amusement parks and entire malls have been known to shut down to allow megastars and their families to entertain themselves without any public distractions. People notice you everywhere you go, and they politely harass you for your autograph and request that you take a picture with them. But you also receive this benefit: the benefit of the doubt from fans and the rest of society.

The rules are broken or bent for us, and we get numerous chances. First-class service is a must, followed by the red carpet being rolled out for us. We get exposure and opportunities most people don't receive and couldn't even imagine. We often get breaks from the police when we are caught speeding. We're always accommodated, and most of us with egos come to expect this type of treatment everywhere we go. And when we don't get it, we take it as disrespect.

But when we are out of the league, or off the stage, and no one is calling our names anymore, most of us can't handle it. Like André 3000, from the hip hop duo known as Outkast, once said, "You can't be the king of the parking lot forever." Consequently, we often turn to other things to handle the depression (woman, drugs, alcohol, pills, or new ways to get ourselves back in the limelight that's spelled J-A-I-L). We constantly seek validation and that level of recognition that we once had. In short, we are dying to be relevant again. The point is to stop trying to achieve the applause of people and, instead, pursue the approval of God.

## False Idols

Most people don't know there are many nights I still don't sleep. I worry about tomorrow—not about myself necessarily, but mostly about my family. I also worry about extended family, friends, and childhood acquaintances. Truth be told, many of my worries are self-inflicted, as we'll continue to discuss. One problem I want to help you overcome today is the issue of comparing yourself to all the false imagery in our world. To do this, you should always focus on the facts, not the feelings. In other words, you need to quit idolizing people and stop thinking everyone has it great but you. People don't have better lives than other people. They just have a better appreciation of life than other people. I mean, really, what are the chances that you got the only bowl of pudding that didn't have the proof in it? Appearances are deceitful. And believing others have some sort of advantage over you, will only hold you back.

Everyone has challenges, and everyone has private pain. And we all have blessings and opportunities. American author, entrepreneur, philanthropist, and life coach Tony Robbins says, "Pain is a part of life, but suffering is a choice."

## JAG

I prayed my entire life that I wouldn't be a JAG. God knew this was short for "Just Another Guy." As long as I can remember, I never wanted to be an average kid going through grade school, middle school, and high school. I wanted to achieve something great. I wanted to be great. I wanted to make an impact and be remembered forever. I wanted to leave a legacy, and I still do.

God gifted me with opportunities in the game of football and graced me with the athletic ability to become a professional athlete. I didn't have to work for those gifts, because He gave them to me. But I had to work to maintain, develop, and enhance those blessings. The Bible teaches us that God makes room for our gifts. I believe that our gifts, in turn, make the way for our purpose. Subsequently, our gifts and passions will then fund our purpose. If it's God's will, then it's God's bill. If you can afford your dreams, then they're probably just a few really good ideas. Your dreams should always be big and exceed your budget.

Football has allowed me to meet the right people and to be at the right place at the right time so I could walk into my purpose. But if football didn't exist, there's no doubt in my mind that I would still have become very successful at something in life. This is because I was determined not to be a JAG.

What's your definition of success? Is it based on comparison to other people's public profiles? Is fame your finish line? God wants us to be content but not complacent. Success is obtainable to all of us, if we want it bad enough, but significance is God-sent. Significance outlasts our earthly vessels.

## TURNOVERS

- We all make the mistake thinking God needs us to do what He already has done. The truth is, he doesn't need us to save the world a second time.
- We confuse being emotional and vulnerable as a sign of being weak. Lil Wayne said, "Even when a wolf cries, he still shows his teeth." You can find strength in pain.
- We automatically lose when we try to earn praise from people, instead of approval from God.

## TAKEAWAYS

- People only see your glory and don't know your story. Share all of your story with people. The good, the bad, and the ugly. They might not want to hear the bad parts, but they will respect you afterward.
- Focus on the facts, never the emotions.
- Never go through a senseless season. There's always a lesson to be learned in every season you go through, both good and bad. Get every lesson in every season. Profit from the past and invest it in the future.

# Chapter 9

# LEAVE VERSUS CLEAVE

I remember my sophomore year in high school when the very first college recruiter came to visit me. He started his presentation with, "This will be the biggest decision of your young life up until this point. Where you decide to go to college will more than likely lead to you making the biggest and most important decision in your life. Even who you will marry! It's a very high chance that you will find the person with whom you will spend the rest of your life with at the college you attend the next couple of years."

Obviously, at the ripe age of fourteen, marriage was so far from my mind that the recruiter would've been better off communicating with me in Morse code, because I wasn't paying attention to any of that marriage "nonsense." Fast forward to now and, of course, that's exactly what happened. I met my wife, Linda, on her college campus, Florida A&M University, which was walking distance from my campus.

One of my biggest fears and challenges of becoming successful was having to find someone I could trust. Specifically, in dealing with athletes, it's very important for us to find this person we wholeheartedly trust before we become successful. In most cases, many of us try to at least start this search process in high school. We hope to find that person early to assure ourselves that he or she is with us for only the right reasons. One can never be too careful or always get it right, especially when money is involved. Money and fame often highlight or bring out a part of a person that not even Doc Brown from *Back to the Future* could see or predict.

Once you find that special person you want to marry and spend the rest of your life with, instantaneously make it your business to start going to counseling and taking classes to prepare for married life and to learn what God teaches us about marriage. Getting married isn't the hardest part, and I'm willing to bet you think staying married is. But that's also incorrect. Staying *happily* married and growing in your love for the other person are the *real* challenges. For the successful or wealthy partner coming into a relationship with someone who may not be as financially stable at the time, it's very difficult to buy into the "what's mine is hers and what's hers is mine" principle. This can open an entirely different book of problems, and this was something I struggled with for a long time. At times, I'd find myself trying to revert to those old thought patterns. But my wife does a great job of bringing everything we disagree on, or battle over, back to, "What does God say about it?" That's a fight not even Floyd "Money" Mayweather can win.

Consequently, I see why it's easier for wealthy people to marry other wealthy people. I'm not saying I agree with it, but now that I'm more seasoned, I understand the thinking behind it. Marriage can be more relatable and more transparent when both parties have a dog in the fight. With that said, it's very difficult to find a transactional relationship that's also completely transparent. Arranged marriages or strategically joined unions between two wealthy families, or individuals, can also cause major strife and rebellion from all parties involved.

And, I hate to break the news to you, but marriage can't be operated like a Fortune 500 company or treated as an alignment of powers. In other words, marriages based on business decisions usually go out of business rather quickly. Being pressured by your parents to marry rich or to marry a person who has a specialized profession (such as a doctor, lawyer, engineer, or athlete), or to marry someone in a position of power or someone who has a degree of influence is like trying to fit a square peg into a round hole. This kind of control and manipulation by parents leads to major dysfunction within the child's life, causing low self-esteem, lack of self-worth, isolation, hatred, and rebellion toward parents and extended family. Consequently, if a child doesn't follow the family guidelines set by the elders (or should I say whomever is sitting on the throne), the child runs the risk of being cut off, looked down upon, or being labeled the "black sheep" of the family. Being ostracized and persecuted by your loved ones for wanting to chase your own dreams can result in addiction, alcoholism, depression, drug usage, feelings of disconnection, rage, suicide, and not feeling loved or wanted. I could go on, but I'm sure you get my point.

The bad news is you're not going to be liked or fit in with everyone, including your own family.

Good news: The great ones never do. Pearl S. Buck says, "Love cannot be forced, love cannot be coaxed and teased. It comes out of heaven, unasked and unsought." Parents who give their children the good old "does he or she check all your boxes?" speech are setting their children up for a disaster. In using premeditated methods such as these, you strip your child from the truest and most organic experience of nature and life: falling in love.

## Welcome to the Family

Have you ever heard the old saying, "When a man marries a woman, he marries her entire family?" The first time you hear it, it sounds like a joke, and the actual thought of it is kind of funny. But it's far from a joke. And if money is involved, there won't be much laughter.

In so many marriages today, specifically where a bride or groom comes from modest means and marries a wealthy partner, it's no laughing matter at all. The financially blessed partner doesn't realize what they've signed up for until they go through the family initiation process. Or what I like to call the "new family member orientation," which often occurs at the wedding reception. This is where the rich groom or bride gets the privilege or opportunity to meet all the rest of the aunts, uncles, nieces, nephews, and cousins that he or she has never met before. Every family has at least a few of them on the family roster. These are the family members we don't always like to claim or initially introduce to our friends. If you're having problems identifying who that family member is in your own family, then chances are you're that family member. (I am only joking!)

After a few glasses of champagne, some will express exactly how they feel about you joining their family. In other words, what's yours is now hers—and what's hers is now theirs! Before a rich man or woman marries their companion, he or she must first divorce or set healthy boundaries with their immediate families. What the new in-laws fail to realize is that the groom or bride's family will not happily or easily sign the divorce papers to release their loved one to support an extended branch of the family tree. Especially not a new branch that doesn't bleed the same blood or bear the same last name as the rest of the tree.

It's not a coincidence that the words parent and premarital agreement, also known as "prenup," both start with the letter "P." Most parents or family members who feel threatened by the new spouse of their loved one are the driving forces behind

getting a prenuptial agreement signed. This will ease their spirits and make them feel a lot safer knowing that the "cash cow"
is protected if anything goes wrong. Believe me when I say the
immediate family and friends, or "Day Ones," as rapper Drake
refers to them, won't ride off into the sunset without a fight.

## A Different View

Several thousand years ago, God gave the most profound wedding toast ever spoken. Genesis 2:24 states, "Therefore shall a
man leave his father and his mother, and shall cleave unto his
wife: and they shall be one flesh." God was speaking to the first
married couple, Adam and Eve. And, in case you were wondering, "cleave" is an old English word that simply means "join."

Of all the things God could have said to these newlyweds,
He chose to speak about the relationship between a married
couple and their parents. But wait! Adam and Eve didn't even
have earthly parents. God was speaking to them as future parents and talking to all future couples and parents about what
to expect when their sons and daughters get hitched. I'm not
sure what you understood from that Bible verse, but what I got
from the text was this: The only expectation we can truly have
for our children when getting married is to realize they are programmed to leave us.

Marriage is as equally a *cleaving process* as much as it is a *leaving process*. That's because you can't have one without the oth-

er. The most common mistake regarding the leave and cleave process is that most of us do it out of order. I truly believe the cleaving process between a man and woman must begin way before they even begin to think about marriage, which ignites the leaving process. So many of us cleave to our spouses, but we still have not completed—or in some cases even started—the leaving process from our parents. Both processes require intentionality. Both can be challenging, at times, but they can also be very rewarding. When the hearts and the intentions of the immediate family and loved ones are not in line with the principles of what God instructs us to do about marriage, it becomes easy for our families to focus only on what they'll be forfeiting, losing, or sharing, instead of what they'll be gaining.

It can become extremely difficult for a newly married person to make the right shift in boundaries and priorities when it comes to their close friends, siblings, and (especially) their parents. It's new territory for all parties—one that requires new communication skills, patience, selflessness, and, most importantly, understanding. I can honestly say this has, by far, been one of the most challenging obstacles I've had to go through since getting engaged and now being married for several years, due to my role as the provider or Bank of Hope for my family. At times, money can complicate more than it can correct. In general, the more stuff you have, the more stuff you have to worry about.

For example, when the new husband or wife says "no" to an

in-law, it's simple for the in-laws to assume they are being shut out by the spouse from their own child, and there's no way their child has any knowledge of this. It's so easy for the parents to resent or blame the new husband or wife for the change that has taken place in their own son or daughter. The new, but strong, relationship between the newlyweds can also cause jealousy and envy from siblings whom you once shared an inseparable and unbreakable bond with. This has led to many generations of ir-reconcilable mother and daughter-in-law, father and son-in-law, and brother and sister-in-law relationships, on top of so many direct fallouts between immediate family members. In my own life, I suffered one of the worst and most heartbreaking big-sis-ter/baby-brother relationship breakups of all time.

My sister was my best friend for a long time. However, when I got engaged, things changed. Even though I still loved and val-ued my sister, I had a new priority, and I was in a new season of my life. The closer Linda and I got, the more my sister reviled her. This continued to fester over time without me ever respect-fully addressing my sister about the situation. I was cleaving to my future wife, but I hadn't fully completed the leaving process from my parents and, particularly, my sister in this case. As a result, my sister started to be blatantly mean and disrespect-ful to Linda, which, at the time, destroyed any chance of them cultivating a strong relationship. And it almost destroyed the re-lationship between my sister and I to the point of no return. It felt like I had to divorce my sister to marry my wife. Fortunately, there is no such thing, but you get what I am trying to say. There will come a time in every person's life when you'll have to draw a line in the sand and say enough is enough. Hopefully, this occurs sooner rather than later. Or better yet, just nip it in the bud from the very beginning, or it will come back to bite you. Over the years of our marriage, my sister, Linda, and I have treated the wounds and healed completely, but the scars are still there. That's why clear communication and healthy boundaries are so important to be established on the front end.

Couples also need strong conviction about unified boundaries. If a couple isn't on the same page about their extended family, it's easy for a division to creep into the marriage. You must make it very intentional and evident to the blind eye that your spouse is the number one person of importance in your life. The standard of respect and honor should be exemplified by each spouse toward one another, so the rest of the family will understand and know how to treat the in-law. The couple should strive to arrive at a place where their voice is uniform. Everyone within the marriage should always be responsible for handling their own individual side of the family and should always respect their spouse's decisions. This will protect and help save face for your spouse with your family.

To help alleviate any money disputes or fallouts in the future over one spouse's family always needing help or bailouts versus the other, collectively come up with a yearly amount of money you both feel comfortable donating to help either side of the family. Make sure you equally ration out the money in the account until it's depleted. After that, don't feel guilty for choosing to protect yourself and your family's legacy because the extended family isn't concerned about it. You won't be giving up on them, you'll simply be accepting the fact that you can't change them.

As kids growing up, we were drilled and trained to believe there's always a winner and a loser, or that someone always had to be either right or wrong. Instead, I believe our focus should be geared toward teaching and learning how to accept the actions of our loved ones. No matter how hard we try, we can't change others. However, we can learn how to accept others for who they are and still not approve of their actions. Accepting others for who they are doesn't mean we condone their behavior, or that we're winning or losing a battle. In fact, accepting others for who they are falls right in the middle of winning and losing.

## Red Shirts

Speaking of winning and losing, when it comes to our young kids, we should talk about parents who "red-shirt" their four-year-olds. Many parents hold kindergartners back and don't allow them to start school on time, thinking this will give them a competitive edge—academically and athletically. This decision is out of the child's control, but it will affect them for a lifetime. Of course, every case is different and personal. Parents want what's best for their kids. I get it! But, I encourage all parents to make sure they check their motivation in the decision. In other words, be sure you are not trying to manipulate your children for your own potential gain.

## Parent Point

As a parent, you must learn to let your kids grow up. It's imperative that we learn how to transition from leading our children, when they couldn't lead themselves, to loosening up the reins and steering them only when needed. Marriage represents a new chapter in your child's life as well as a new chapter in your relationship with them. Prepare for that day by letting your child practice making decisions and experiencing the consequences of those decisions from an early age.

Don't question the motivations of your child's fiancé when it comes to money and then operate with the same questionable motives. Start evaluating yourself and create healthy boundaries from the beginning. Ask yourself how you would respond if you were in your child's shoes. How would you want the relationship with *your* parents and *your* in-laws to be? As a man, I often remind myself that every man wants a woman to love them unconditionally, always put them first, serve them, give them the utmost respect, and treat them like a king. On that same note, women desire a man who will cherish, honor, love, protect, respect, value, and treat them like a queen. I can't expect anything different from the young man who attempts to date or marry my daughter. If he does not expect those same things from his future wife, then he isn't the one for my daughter. And if my daughter doesn't learn from the example I set with how I treat her mother, and she allows a man to treat her differently, it's her fault. You see how easy it is for us to place our expectations on others, especially when it's someone we love and care deeply about.

Also, consider if money is influencing your emotions and behavior. Remember, money isn't evil, but the *love* of money is the root of all evil. Without large amounts of money being involved, parents are ecstatic, happy, and delighted to give their children away—all for the simple reason of passing the responsibility of their children onto someone else.

A wise man once shared with me that the first step of a parent becoming a free person again is when their child reaches the age of eighteen. The second step is when that same child turns twenty-one. The final and last step is when they get married. But, we all know if that same child is wealthy, things are drastically different from the parent's point of view. Why so? God's word about marriage didn't change. The Bible taught us as parents to prepare for this day and to expect for our seeds to leave us and to cleave to their spouses. So, where did all these new expectations and entitlements come from?

The short, and not-so-sweet, answer is that they come from our own selfish desires. This is why it's very important for you to have your own life, your own job, and your own money. If not, you'll think everyone that your son or daughter brings home is after their money—or, should I say, the money they normally give you. The thought of your allowance or your child's over-flow being cut off scares you and can result in you acting out of character, forcing you to go into self-preservation mode because you can feel someone's hands in your pockets. From this point, everyone becomes a threat to the throne. If you aren't willing to step up and do what's necessary for you to provide for yourself, and you choose to continue to depend on your child, watch out world. Because no one is safe!

As a parent, ask yourself if you appreciated your mother or father's relationship with your spouse. If the relationship had healthy boundaries, honor those with your child. If not, make a change for the sake of your family and legacy. My wife and my parents always had a solid relationship from my point of view. My parents never questioned Linda's love for me. They also never got involved in our relationship when we were dating. They allowed nature to run its course when it came to Linda and me getting married. Over the years of us being married, my mom and Linda have created a special bond to where my mom calls her to check on me, being that I'm not a huge phone guy. I could see the relationship growing between my wife and my mom back in my college days. My wife's mom, unfortunate-ly, passed away when Linda was a young girl. So, my mom, from day one, has filled that role for her. It's been great to watch and even see where the roles have been reversed to where my mom calls on Linda for advice.

## Men, Marriage, and Mom

Marriage represents a massive shift in relationships and responsibility. There's a new number one in your life, and, for the first
time, it's not your mom—or, as in my case, your sister. My sister
and I had a genuine, organic, strong, and unique relationship
growing up. It really began to flourish and take form as I went
off to college and my parents started to lose respect and trust
from us. As siblings, we had to depend on each other and to
have each other's backs. The fact of Linda taking her place and
being moved to the front seat of my life, did not sit well with my
sister at all. I touched on that story earlier, so I will stay focused
on men and their relationship with their moms.

This shift is easier said than done. For most little boys, moms
are our first crush. We completely adore, love, respect, and place
our moms on pedestals. There's no greater love for a child than
their love for their mother. It's truly a special bond. Remember,
in the first book of the Bible, we're told that marriage means
leaving and joining. However, leaving doesn't mean abandoning
or isolating yourself from your family. In Exodus 20:12, we're
told that honoring your mother and father are on God's Top
10 list.

It's not only possible to honor your parents as a married
man, God also promises a blessing to those who do. Marriage

represents a change in relationship and, most importantly, a change in priorities. Look at it as a changing of the guards or that a new sheriff is in town. And this applies to all members of your immediate family.

But, like everyone else in this world, no one likes change. People will claw, scratch, fight, kick, and manipulate to keep change from happening. It's very difficult to effect change if you haven't been infected by change. The simple words from the Bible contain profound wisdom for those who will listen and act. As always, God's commands are not intended to be a burden or to cause division. Instead, they are to save us from unnecessary burdens in our relationships. God is trying to spare us some pain through some tough love and straight talk. God loves you, and God loves marriage.

## Leave and Cleave or Deal with the Mess

Leaving and cleaving creates new situations. And new situations demand decisions. And these decisions can't be put off until later. Like one of the most successful coaches in all of sports history, UCLA Men's Basketball Coach John Wooden, said, "If you don't have time to do it right from the start, when will you have time to do it over?"

Here's a principle about cleaving or joining. It won't make every decision easy, but it will help you make the right decision:

First and foremost, always be in agreement with the one you're joined to. In other words, dance with the person you came to the party with. Learn to live by this lesson, and you'll always receive a blessing.

My wife and I often discuss difficult situations. When I follow this principle of agreement, it's amazing how good situations turn out in the end. (And when I haven't followed this principle, it's amazing how . . . well, you know.) If you can't come to an agreement, don't be in a hurry to decide. Just remember: Too much analysis leads to paralysis.

## Your New Team

When I went from playing for the Seminoles to joining the Steelers, I was in a new city with new teammates and new rules, but my expectations and standards never changed. When I left the Steelers to go play for the Titans, it was the same. I was in a different city, with different teammates and different rules, but my expectations and standards never changed. At the end of the day, no matter where I was, whether it be Seminole Country, "Bliztburgh," or in the Music City, my standards of excellence and commitment to winning never changed. But, to achieve this, I always had to respect my new team and put them first. On each specified date, my time was up and I had to leave the Seminoles, then the Steelers, and join the Titans. From that day forward, I had a new uniform, a new home, a new mission, and a new football family.

Will everyone like the change? Not at all. I've heard words like, "You only care about your new family, and you're not thinking about my family!" and "You're just like all the other athletes who make it big. You make your money and forget about your family, and your wife's family gets to enjoy it all, while the people who were with you from the start get the leftovers." Yes, and I hope you feel the same about providing for *your* family.

Will the new decisions be easy? Of course not. Is cleaving worth it? Absolutely. Will clear boundaries eventually be a blessing to every member of your family, both immediate and extended? Yes, eventually. The same holds true with your friendships. To be successful at this, we have to find the strength to overcome the things that try to overcome us.

# TURNOVERS

- From now on, when you dream, see the entire picture. As a kid, when we had dreams about being able to take care of our parents, siblings, and families, a wife or husband wasn't in those dreams. Start incorporating a wife or husband in your dreams so you'll be prepared for it when the time comes, and you'll know how to operate within those boundaries.

- We attempt to cleave to our wives or husbands without first leaving our parents and families. This is out of order and will cause serious problems later down the road.

- Trying to control our kids by dictating their moves and being too involved in their marriage will backfire. Don't make your child choose between you and their spouse when it comes to who is number one in their lives.

- As parents, we make the mistake of not preparing for the day that our children will meet Mr. or Mrs. Right to take our places. As a result, it can be hard for us to let them go.

# TAKEAWAYS

- Marriage is a cleaving process as much as it is a leaving process. Parents, step outside of your selfishness and recognize your child and their spouse want to put each other first.

- Establish clear and healthy boundaries for your family before your spouse feels disrespected or offended by your family. Set the tone on how your family is to treat your wife or husband.

- Everyone in the marriage should be responsible for handling their own side of the family. Have one song and be one voice. Always protect each other from one another's family.

# Chapter 10

# HEADS VERSUS TAILS

I have participated in a few coins tosses in my days. It's a big part of the game. Simple, but very important. Let's just say, even though the coin used during the coin toss isn't worth much, the toss itself carries a lot of weight.

Wikipedia defines coin flipping as "the practice of throwing a coin in the air to choose between two alternatives, sometimes to resolve a dispute between two parties. It's a form of solution which inherently has only two possible and equally likely outcomes."

Flipping a coin, or choosing heads or tails, is supposed to be a simple, noncompetitive, and unbiased way to decide between two options. Several sports, including most forms of football, cricket, and volleyball, include this method to help determine which end of the field the teams will play on and which team will get possession of the ball first.

The point is to have fairness and equality to avoid a conflict. We can clearly see and understand why this method works so well in sports and other forms of competition. However, we're only setting ourselves up for failure and disappointment when we desire for our relationships to work this way. Oh, how easy life would be if we could just settle our differences by flipping a coin! I stated earlier that the world is 100 percent occupied with imperfect people, so trying to discover true perfection is a lost cause.

So, as much as I hate to say it, and as much as I would love for it to be true, relationships can't be viewed in just black and white. Which means that intense, heartfelt conversations cannot be *totally* settled by a simple coin toss. However, relationships and passionate conversations can be examined and settled by using facts. Only facts, I might add. Try your best to eliminate all emotions and stick strictly to the facts. Before it all goes down, remember to call out heads or tails loud enough for everyone to hear what side you are on. Depending on how the outcome affects you, there's a high probability you will want to change sides or ask for the coin to be flipped again.

## The Flip Side

Off the field, heads or tails decisions are far different. There's a weight that comes with leadership and an even larger accountability and responsibility that comes with being able to bless someone. Being a good steward of what God has blessed you with is so much bigger than money or just handing money out to those in need. The dictionary defines stewardship as the overseeing and protection of something considered worth caring for and protecting.

We are merely stewards and not owners of our stuff. Let's not confuse ownership with stewardship. We are only managers of what God has blessed us with. In other words, we can have and enjoy the fruits, but we can't have the tree. There are no explanations or limitations on what God chooses to bless us with, so we can't expect any explanations or limitations on what God chooses to withhold from us.

Since we don't really own anything, we don't get to call the shots. We have to stop taking credit for what God has done for us in our lives. That's spiritual plagiarism. Everything we have belongs to God, and He only gives us what we can be trusted with. Our gifts are never bestowed for our own glory but always for His glory. God doesn't instruct me to help everyone in need every single time, which leaves a heavy burden of guilt on my heart.

Growing up, I often heard many leaders express their concerns and dislikes about the huge penalty and pressure that comes with being a leader. "A good leader is a person who takes a little more than his share of the blame and a little less than his share of the credit," says John Maxwell. And Hall of Fame player and coach Dick LeBeau, my defensive coordinator when I played for the Pittsburgh Steelers, is an excellent example of being a great leader. When we won and played well on defense, Coach LeBeau always gave the players all the credit, praise, and recognition. On the other hand, when we lost a game or one of the few times we didn't play well as a defense, Coach LeBeau took all the blame. That's exactly why every time Coach LeBeau took off for a walk or sat down to eat lunch, he was always surrounded by players and other coaches. If you think you're a good leader, all you have to do is start walking. If you don't see anyone behind you, there's your answer. You're not leading. You're just taking a walk.

As I've learned for myself, there's no truer saying than, "Experience is the best teacher." In Luke 12:48, the Bible says, "To whom much is given, much is required." Depending on your status in life, the world holds different, and sometimes very biased, expectations on you. Or in layman's terms, the world has a funny way of just picking up and moving the finish line. As a result, I interpret that verse as saying, "To whom much is given, much more is required."

For example, why is okay for the poor to call the rich snobby, stuck up, and selfish, but the rich can't call the poor lacking, lazy, and luckless? And, why is it okay for someone to remind the successful person of all the things they've done to help the successful person get to where they are in life, but when the successful person starts to remind that same person how many times they've helped them, it's hurtful, insincere, and rude?

If you're successful, you may have heard some of these:

- "I used to drive you to practice."
- "I bought you a certain pair of shoes."
- "I always took you to get your haircut."
- "I used to look out for you."
- "I sacrificed a lot for you."
- "I worked two and sometimes three jobs to buy you clothes for Christmas."
- "If it wasn't for me, you wouldn't be where you are today."

The list goes on and on. But when a successful person reminds family and friends about all the ways he or she has helped them, the response from them goes something like the following:

- Why are you keeping tabs on what you have done for me?
- Why are you still living in the past?
- Why are you throwing what you did for me back up in my face?
- How long are you going to hold that over my head?
- I thought you were just helping me out!
- Helping each other out is what families do.
- Are you really counting that?
- I just always expected you to do that for me!

- Do you remember what I used to do for you, or did you forget?

And I'd be remiss if I didn't share a few of the Hall of Fame responses:

- Why aren't you just giving from your heart?
- If it's not from your heart, I'd rather you not give it to me or do it for me.
- I'd rather go without, if I knew I had to get subpoenaed for asking for some money.
- I never thought I would have to ask my multimillionaire son, daughter, brother, or sister for anything.
- If I had the money, you would never have to ask or worry about anything.

Two different sides of the same coin, right? Based on my own experiences with this, I have to wonder about the following:

- Why can a family member tell a successful person how they feel about a situation or exactly what is on their mind, but when the person with the money expresses the same freedom of speech, it's taken as being bossy or being a dictator?
- Why is it that when a successful person steps up and voices his or her feelings in a respectful manner, the

other person feels as if they are being controlled and overpowered, due to the fact the successful person is paying all the bills?

- Why is it that when the person with the money decides to ask a question or do a little investigating on where his or her money is going, the recipient of the money reacts angrily and gets defensive?

- Why do people borrow money from you with a smile, and (if and) when they pay you back, they do it with an attitude?

It seems to me, those who borrow money from us want us to listen without responding. They want us to give without asking what the money will be used for. To lend money without expecting to get paid back. And to purchase someone a home or car without telling them how to take care of it. It seems to me that signing up for all of that is a bit of a fool's errand. So, I'll leave those of you thinking of borrowing money with some food for thought: Before borrowing money from a friend, decide which one you need the most.

It's very healthy and positive for all parties involved to assess ourselves and our situations, regardless of what side of the coin we're on. We can't fix our situations until we face them. We have to own our own stuff and stop blaming everyone else around us. Also, it's important to manage your expectations so that they are truly reciprocal. For example, don't expect me to do or tolerate something from you that you wouldn't do or tolerate from me. Also, don't ask me for anything I can't ask you for, whether it's money or anything else.

If you ask my wife, one of my biggest pet peeves in life is when a person asks someone to do something they have either not done themselves or they are not willing to do. I can vividly see and hear, on several different occasions, a friend of mine arguing and fussing with someone over some money the person owed them. I mean it got so ugly over the phone, I was afraid to see what would happen when they finally bumped into each other. I'm not judging them, because I completely understand their position.

The only issue I had was with the statement my friend made to me after hanging up the phone. He said, "I can't stand it when people see you and know they owe you money but act like everything is all good!" If only he recognized and knew how I was feeling in that very moment, with him owing me three times as much money as the person he was fussing with over the phone owed him, he probably would've kept that comment to himself. But, what he was really saying to me was, "Since Chris already has money, the thought of me paying him back is the least of my worries." What he failed to realize was that we both came from the same struggle, same city, and same humble beginnings, which is one of the main reasons we were good friends. We understood each other and were both cut from the same cloth. He failed to consider that the amount of money in my account did not change the DNA of who I am.

This reminds me of the parable found in Matthew 18:23-35, with the story of a servant who owed his master 10,000 bags of gold but was not able to repay him. So, he begged his master for mercy and asked his master to have patience with him, in hopes that one day he would be able to pay him back in full. Instead of his master selling off his wife and children to pay off his debt, his master had compassion for him and canceled his debt, only for that same servant to go out and find one of his fellow servants who owed him only 100 silver coins and immediately applied pressure on him to repay his debt. He choked his fellow servant and demanded him to pay him back what he owed. His fellow servant begged for mercy, patience, and more time to one day pay him back as well. However, he refused to show compassion for his fellow servant and threw him into prison until he could pay off the debt. When the master heard about what happened, he called the servant back in and put him in jail and tortured him, because he failed to grant his fellow servant the same compassion, grace, and mercy he had just received.

## Heads or Tails

If you are blessed to be on the so-called "good side" of the coin, would you allow your loved ones to take advantage of you by playing on your emotions? Is this double standard fair? Of course, it isn't, but we must deal with reality. A time will come when we all end up on the wrong side of the coin. When that time comes, we must be careful to avoid this dual standard ourselves. And, just for the record, it won't always be about money issues.

For example, when your child starts playing sports, and he or she is getting a lot of playing time, or is the star of the team, the coach is the greatest and smartest coach ever. But, when your child starts playing less for whatever reason, you might find yourself thinking, *"It's a terrible school that needs a new coach—and my child needs to transfer!"* Tell me you haven't witnessed this before. If not, you haven't kept your child enrolled at one school long enough for someone to catch you saying it.

It's always funny to hear how easily and quickly someone tells me to say no when I ask for their advice or opinion on whether I should help someone else in need. Then, two days later, that same person finds themselves in a similar situation, and they can now tell me all the reasons why I should help them and how their situation is so much different. As Anaïs Nin said, "We don't always see things as they are, we see things as we are."

Without careful reflection and consideration of others, we can only see one side of a coin at a time—whatever side we are looking at or currently standing on. So, take the time to look at both sides of any challenging situation. A healthy relationship tries to understand the other side before forming an opinion and then still doesn't judge.

There are three types of people:

- Those who see you winning and look to you to make them a winner.
- Those who see you winning and look to you for inspiration and advice as they work to become a winner.
- Those who just flat-out want to win and will do so by any means necessary.

When life happens to us, and we are faced with a huge dilemma, simply toss a coin. It not only works, it also clears up any confusion we may have. That's because in that brief moment, while the coin is flipping in the air, we know—and loudly voice—what we are wishing for. Or in other words, we know what side of the coin we are on. It's important to understand the difference for yourself before you toss any more coins around.

## TURNOVERS

- We foolishly and irresponsibly bless our family and friends, in hopes that blessings will come from our generosity.
- We make the mistake of sowing good seeds into bad ground.
- To whom much is given, much is required. We allow our families and friends to take advantage of us. Hold everyone in your inner circle accountable for the role they play.

## TAKEAWAYS

- If you think you're being a good leader, just stop walking, turn around, and look behind you. If you don't see anybody following you, you're only taking a walk. Learn to take all the blame and none of the credit.
- If you can't afford to offer a gift, then you can't afford to give it away.
- Before you start criticizing and judging, put on the other person's shoes and see from their view. Bishop T. D. Jakes says, "Giraffes and turtles have different views. Don't let a turtle give you advice about your giraffe vision. A turtle can only report from its level. You cannot get a turtle to understand a giraffe decision."

# Chapter 11

# PLAYOFFS

As I look back over my college career, I played in three straight national championships, captured four ACC titles in a row, won a lot of games, and played for the legendary coach Bobby Bowden. I also had the privilege of being coached by Mickey Andrews, a legend in his own right, who was the defensive coordinator and defensive back coach during FSU's years of dominance on the defensive side of the ball. I will still, to this day, run through a wall for that man. Or at least try to!

During my four years at FSU, my mental strength began to match the altitude of my physical strength. Not just because I was surrounded by great coaches and so many amazing athletes, but mainly because I had no choice. I was all alone. I had to really grow up mentally, and do it quickly, because going back home empty-handed was not an option for me. Plus, I really didn't have a home to go back to anyway. At least not the one I grew up in. Unfortunately, we lost my childhood home during my junior or senior year in college. Forgive me for not knowing the exact year, but when you try to hold onto only the good memories and forget some, or at least most, of the bad ones, time starts running together.

When you first go off to college, it's just you. Depending on where you attend college and how far it is from your hometown, there's a good chance you'll be a lone ranger. You won't have anyone looking over your shoulder, you won't have anyone making sure you do the right thing, and you won't have anyone waking you up every morning to make sure you attend class every day. So, your attention to detail and focus must be intense and laser sharp. Especially when you don't have a safety net or stable supporting cast back home to help keep you encouraged and motivated when times become more challenging.

I felt like college was my moment—my chance to break through. My opportunity to manufacture change. Change is never just about a matter of ability, but it's always about a matter of motivation. I couldn't afford to mess up this opportunity. All the answers to the test, the clues to my quest, and the treasures in my hidden chest were all at FSU now. I already knew what was back home in Rock Hill waiting for me, so time was of the essence. I had no room for error or extra time for a do-over. I made up my mind: I was going to be stronger than my strongest excuse.

I graduated in just three and a half years, *summa cum laude*, (which stands for highest honors, or what my dad thought to be a last name at my brother's graduation a few years prior). What an unforgettable and hysterical moment in the Hope family. This is a story that will be passed down from generation to generation. My family redefined the meaning of laughter and embarrassment for my brother that day in the audience as we sat and watched his graduation. My dad, after hearing *"cum laude"* repeated at the end of so many students' last names as they marched across the stage, actually thought it was a popular or common last name for people where my brother attended college. Out of nowhere my dad loudly whispers, "Damn, it sure is a lot of them Cum Laude people graduating today! They must have some strong genes. They must be pretty smart too, because ain't no way a parent could afford to send all of them kids to college at the same time!" The irony of his comments, let alone being blessed enough to witness that in person, still makes me cry from breathtaking laughter every time I hear someone tell that story.

In college, I remember going to parties and coming home early to study—or studying first and then going to parties later. Sometimes, I'd get to the club in just enough time to catch what we used to refer to as the "let-out." The let-out was a term we used to describe the perfect timing of when the doors of the club would open to let the partygoers out of the club. If carefully calculated and planned correctly, you could get there in such a fashion that most people wouldn't know whether or not you were actually inside the club before it closed. I mean my teammates and I would have the discussion earlier in the day of whether we were going to the actual club or just catching the let-out! I mean, either way, you had to get dressed, figure out who was driving, and come to the realization it was going to be a long night and an early morning.

There were a lot of benefits of just attending the let-out. First of all, it could save you some money, on gas at least, because we never really had to pay to get into the clubs anyway. Secondly, it could save your shoes from being stepped on all night and your clothes from smelling like smoke or being sweated out from being in a hot, packed club. Thirdly, it saved you from being stuck in traffic when leaving the club, because you normally had to park farther away than normal due to all the cars of the people already inside the club. Back then, we didn't have a clue about valet parking, nor did we have the money to pay for it. And besides, a little extra walking never hurt anyone, especially not a five-star athlete. I never heard anyone complain about the short walk to the club. Or, at least, they never complained about it around me. And lastly, in my case, it allowed me to get my school work done and still not miss any of the action. I could get my nerd on and my mac on, all at the same time, and no one ever knew. So, it was a win-win for me.

I share all of this to let you know I could've easily allowed so many distractions, including good-intentioned ones, to keep me looking back on the negative experiences from my past and delay me from getting to where I needed to go. But, I wanted what I was chasing after so badly that I was willing to sacrifice for it and not allow anything to get in my way from having it. In the quiet moments of our decisions is when our destiny is shaped. I am proud to say I'm still the same way today.

## Big League Focus

During my long tenure in the National Football League, each week we faced a different opponent, which presented a different challenge—collectively and individually. Some weeks were more physically demanding while others were very challenging mentally. In most cases in the NFL, the level of talent between players isn't really that much different—all the players compete and perform at a high level. Everyone is strong, big, fast, and athletic. The teams that win the most usually have a few superior players, but, more importantly, they have the mind-set of a winner and a standard of excellence. I've always been programmed with the mind-set of a winner. Like Tony Robbins says, "Winners anticipate, while losers react." That's because true winners only worry about winning, and they allow the losers to focus on losing. I'm a firm believer that good teams find ways to win and losing teams find ways to lose.

The NFL battle doesn't just start on Sunday when the ball is kicked off. It actually starts on Monday when the first meeting begins and the practice for the week starts. Actually, I take that back. Winning really starts in the off-season when preparing for the OTAs, which is short for Organized Team Activities, and the minicamps, and then again during the dreadful, scorching hot, brutal days of training camp. The countless hours of film study, note-taking, weight training, conditioning, and treatment can begin to weigh on any player's focus—even for those like myself who deeply enjoyed and loved what I did for a living. There's an old saying, "Those who bleed more in preparation, bleed less in war."

The battle begins in the mind, then it starts to creep down into each individual part of your body. We have all heard, and in some way or another applied the phrase, "mind over matter." I truly believe that if it doesn't affect your mind, then it won't matter to your body. Waking up early every day, taking the same route to work, eating the same breakfast, seeing the same people, sitting in the same long, boring meetings, and hearing the same voices stand before you and deliver the plan all perpetuate the same monotonous routine. Then, the physical pain of the game starts to join in and have its way with you. As a professional, you really must figure out how to plan, prepare, preserve, and still produce. In other words, welcome to the life in the big leagues. This is also why we get paid the big bucks.

## There Is No Off-Season

A dear cousin of mine once said to me, "You guys have to battle for seventeen weeks out of the year, and if you're good enough, your team will have a chance to play in the playoffs and maybe make it to the Super Bowl. But, when you lose, the season is over, and you get to sit back, kick your feet up, and enjoy the fruits of your labor."

My poor cousin thought he had it all figured out. Contrary to popular belief, in football, or any other sport, when attempting to live a "holy" lifestyle, when pursuing a successful career, or simply just playing this game that we all call "life," the work is never done. There's always so much more for us to improve on and even more for us to learn. One will quickly realize there are really no "off days" for anyone who desires to be great and maintain it. There are fifty-two weeks and fifty-two Sundays in a year, and, very much like the doors at church on Sundays, you always have to be open for business.

Life is made up of daily battles between you and the enemy, the flesh and the spirit. Unfortunately, there's no film to watch or game plan to study that will show you how the enemy plans to attack you next. If you're going to achieve, maintain, and enjoy success, it's imperative you learn how to focus. For example:

- When your mind and body scream at you to stop, you need to focus even harder.
- When friends and family go "out of bounds," you need to focus.
- If you want big-league success, you must practice big-

league focus.

- Learn to starve your distractions and feed your focus.
- The goal is to make it to the playoffs, but the reward is to win the Super Bowl.

We've spelled out the potential pitfalls in pursuing your dreams. Now, it's time to develop a successful game plan to help you break free, accomplish your goals, keep your peace, and get the big "W." Mark Twain said, "Twenty years from now you will be more disappointed by the things you didn't do than by the ones you did do."

## TURNOVERS

- When we take our eyes off the prize, we become distracted and miss out on our breakthrough.
- If you prioritize your time, you'll have enough time to do everything you want to do and not have to risk missing anything—especially the important things.
- We must learn to adjust our mind-sets, because that's where winning and losing begins. Let the losers worry about losing. Big things don't happen with small prayers.

## TAKEAWAYS

- There are no days off! Always be open for business. If you don't like what you see, just change the channel. You're the only one who controls the remote to your life.
- Be stronger than your strongest excuse. Refuse to give up or be denied.
- You must have laser-sharp focus and pay close attention to all the details. You can't afford to take your eyes off the prize and risk missing out on a life-altering opportunity simply because you were distracted.

# Chapter 12

# KNOWING WHERE YOU'RE GOING VERSUS FORGETTING WHERE YOU CAME FROM

To this day, whenever I go home to visit my family in Rock Hill, the first thing my dad does when he sees me is size me up. I think he initially started doing this my freshman year when I came home from college for the very first time. It was during summer break, after being away for months. After he was done sizing me up, he proudly walked away but loudly reminded me, "A young man might have the back, but the old man knows the way!"

I still can vividly remember playing in my first tackle football game. I had just turned seven years old. I was a great size, and I had good speed and a nice skill set for my age, but I had zero game experience. One Saturday morning, on a perfect day for football, my older brother and his Pop Warner teammates racked up a big lead on the team we were playing against. As a result, the park's league rules kicked into play. The rules stated that if a team has a three-touchdown lead on another team, the team with the lead is required to put in their second-string play-ers to sort of even the playing field. So, our coach was forced to put me and a few of the other younger players in the game. Boy, was I excited. I didn't feel nervous, and I was so far from being scared it made me start to think I was a little crazy. I was just super hyped to be playing in a *real* football game.

I had no idea our coach was going to let me run the foot-ball. Please, let me remind you, outside of practice, or every day and every weekend of sandlot football in our neighborhood, this handoff would be the very first time I ever touched the ball in a real live football game. Our coach called the play, and we broke the huddle. Believe it or not, we all lined up correctly without any problems, which was amazing now that I look back on it. The quarterback took the snap from the center, and he handed me the football. I broke through the line of scrimmage like I'd been shot out of a cannon and quickly headed toward the end zone.

In my mind, I was thinking, "Wow, this is pretty cool and very easy!" I couldn't believe what was happening. Just a few more yards and I would score my first real touchdown on my first carry in live action! I can't make this stuff up, people. I'm sure you're probably thinking you could guess what happened next, right?

Just as I was about to cross the goal line and score my first career touchdown, I felt a tug on my arm, and a player from the other team ripped the football away from me in just a matter of seconds before I crossed over into the Promised Land. Instead of scoring my first touchdown, I fumbled the ball through the back of the end zone for what is called a T-O-U-C-H-B-A-C-K, not a T-O-U-C-H-D-O-W-N. It was so disappointing! Touchback and touchdown are very close in terms of their sound, but their meanings are as far away from each other as the beginning and ending points of a never-ending line. Scoring a touchdown makes you famous and puts points on the scoreboard for your team. Scoring a touchback, however, makes you infamous and not only does it take points off the scoreboard for your team, it also gives your opponents possession of the football. The real question is: Will you score, or will you fumble?

## Scoring Versus Fumbling

This is your opportunity. Yes, you know where you came from, but do you know where you're going? And even if you know where you're going, will you reach your goal, or will you have it stripped away? Our goal in life should be to not only achieve success, but also to fully enjoy it as God intended. So, let's talk about turning things around with a new mind-set and creating forward momentum.

My Grandmother Louise used to say, "Everybody wants to go to heaven, but no one wants to die." In other words, everyone wants the prize, but not everyone wants to pay the price. Some people get upset when a friend or family member is running forward and might be slightly out in front of them. Instead of doing what is necessary for them to catch up to the one ahead and score their own touchdowns in the game of life, they would much rather watch that person slip and fall—or, they might even trip the person from behind and strip the ball from their hands, as they fall to the ground.

Life tips: First and foremost, be sure everyone in your boat is rowing. Secondly, make sure they're rowing in the same direction as you are and not against the current. And lastly, make sure they're not drilling holes in your boat when you're not looking. Know your circle.

The reality is, not everyone, including some of your closest family members and friends, are meant to go with you. Relationships serve certain purposes in our lives. Everyone who's connected to you isn't necessarily going to your final destination. When a rocket launches into outer space, the two rocket boosters are very necessary and required to help get the rocket to maximum velocity, so it can reach its highest altitude. But, as the rocket goes higher and ascends to a certain level, the two boosters fall off.

Some people in your life are boosters to get you into your orbit. They are not meant to stay with you all the way up. Stop crying over, or worrying about, people that God has purposely released out of your life. Keep ascending, and don't force people to go where they were never meant to go. It could be very costly for you—and catastrophic in the end.

Often, it's not the actual person who becomes rich that forgets where he or she came from. It's that some people who get rich grow tired of dealing with the old mind-sets of the people from where they come from. And, if we're being completely honest, the individuals surrounding the successful person are really the people whose attitudes have changed.

Whenever a person doesn't understand something, they'll never be able to "stand under" that way of thinking. So, until those same people walk in the successful person's shoes, they'll never understand it. I know what you're thinking. This needs to be looked at from both sides. The successful or rich person needs to walk in the shoes of the other person as well. On many occasions, they already have. Most people who are successful (or that now have money) weren't born into it.

One of the most harmful mind-sets is believing that money can buy happiness. I once had a coach in Pittsburgh tell me, "Money can't buy you happiness, but it will buy you something so close you won't be able to tell the difference." While that may be true in some respects—and a small part of me still agrees with my old coach—I now know for a fact that happiness of that nature isn't everlasting. Standup comedian and actor, Jim Carrey exclaims, " I hope everybody could get rich and famous and will have everything they ever dreamed of, so they will know that it's not the answer."

In Ecclesiastes 5:9-12, the Bible expresses to us that riches alone will never bring us satisfaction and peace. We've all fallen victim to the idea that with more money in our accounts, we'll be able to sleep better at night. Truth be told, money can only solve money problems. We put all our faith and belief in money, thinking it will solve all our problems, but we won't do what our money tells us to do. Our currency clearly reads in big letters, "In God We Trust." It does not say anywhere for us to put our trust in our money or others. I'm a living witness that the number of zeros and commas in your bank account doesn't automatically equate to true peace and happiness. In fact, Tony Robbin says, "Success without fulfillment is the ultimate failure in life." This is because we must learn to stop focusing solely on achievements. Instead, we need to reprogram our minds to chase the experience of fulfillment.

My great friend, former teammate, and future Hall of Famer, Troy Polamulo expressed, "Chris, you've figured out that reversing the cycle isn't a merit-based system but a deep personal inner struggle to reverse a cycle of learned environmental behaviors. Because we have been able to peak our heads into a world that they (family) have yet personally experienced, it's hard for us to point it out because it in turn exposes those whom we love the most. But in order for them to experience it like we have (real success), we all have to be willing to address this pattern of dysfunctional behavior that we all suffer from."

As a college football player, I daydreamed often about the moment when I would hear my name being called by the NFL commissioner during the draft. In my little immature mind, I just knew everything after that moment was going to be perfect with my family again. I assumed the lack of money was the main cause of all the stress and strife between my parents. I had this false expectation that money would restore my parent's relationship and that we'd go back to being like the Huxtable family again—only this time it would be authentic and last.

I also thought the saying, "Money can't buy happiness," was just a myth to make us all feel better about ourselves for not having money, but it's actually very accurate and true. Money can buy you a big house, a new car, and even change your physical appearance, but money can't put a down payment on the most important thing in life—a new mind-set. Only God can give us true joy and happiness.

A closed-minded person with a negative mind-set will try to make you think it's better to be in jail, caged like an animal, getting fed three times a day, and sleeping on a box mattress, than being in the free world where you can create your own destiny. A jacked-up mind-set will persuade you to focus only on the negative, instead of being grateful for the many blessings you have. An unhealthy mind-set will cause you to miss your blessings and ignore the fact that everything you have prayed to God for, He has already blessed you with. Sadly, you just can't see it, because you aren't in the right mental space to receive it.

Most of all, a negative mind-set will keep you blinded by your past, instead of helping you focus on your future. Our past doesn't have anything to do with our future, unless we decide to stay there. It's very important that you take a mental inventory of those closest to you as well. "You did not become who you are in an instant. Instead, you went through a process." Consequently, according to Chris Jackson, you will not discover who you are in an instant, but rather through a process. Therefore, be very careful of the company you keep. There is an old saying: "If you show me a person's friends, I can show you that person's future."

Don't allow the pressure from those who are comfortable where they are and have no desire for anything better in life to deter you from continuing to chase after your goals and dreams. Continue to outgrow and think outside of your box. Stop thinking of ways to find comfort inside your box. I once heard Warren Buffet say, "The chains of habits are too light to be felt, until they are too heavy to be broken."

## Knowing Where You're Going

David Green, philanthropist and a founder of Hobby Lobby, once asked an audience, "What are you doing today that will impact the world a thousand years from now? If your impact is only for today, you're probably not making that big of an impact." Like David Green, I am going for legacy, significance, and impact. Only the people who don't fully understand my vision will say I'm forgetting where I come from.

My wife used to ask me, "So, how much money would it take for you to have in the bank for you to truly relax? How is it that money is still your motivation?" And I would explain to her how our lives are so much bigger than ourselves. One of my biggest goals in life is to create, establish, and maintain financial freedom, because I want our grandkids and great grandkids to be born millionaires. I explained to her the difference between rich and wealthy and the fact that I desire wealth for the future generations of our family. At times, even she didn't understand my motivation. But, I can honestly say that I haven't forgotten where I came from. I'm just focused on where I'm trying to go with my family's finances. I haven't turned my back on my family and friends, and I'm not being selfish. What my wife and I are choosing to do is for our children and future generations.

Mickey Andrews, my college defensive back coach, would always share stories and lessons with us about what he had learned from watching the National Geographic Channel. He loved the idea of survival of the fittest and how animals were blessed with amazing adaptability traits. One day before practice, he shared a story with us about the different animals in the zoo and how the architects of the zoo purposely built the walls slightly above the animal's heads and eyes. Most of the animals in the zoo are born and equipped with the ability to easily jump the wall at any time, but they'll never do it, because they can't see what's on the other side. So many of us are paralyzed by that same fear of the unknown. The only difference is we're not physically trapped inside a fence. We're mentally enclosed by the imaginary fence of fear. Faith and fear are both dealing with the unknown, but faith is positively directed.

There's an old African proverb that says, "If there is no enemy within, then there is no enemy on the outside that can do us any harm." We are our own worst enemy. There's no greater enemy than the enemy in me. Our minds are either our greatest enemies or our greatest allies. When you know where you are going and you know your capabilities, your mind-set will easily change. We'll never be able to progress to our promise if we continue to regress in our past. We must not remain prisoners of our past. We must profit from our past and invest in our future. Unfortunately, there will be people who try to hold you back, and it so happens that sometimes it will be the people closest to you. They'll make you feel guilty for wanting more. Not everyone will be for your success—once you experience it.

Some people want to push you out into success. Yet, at the same time, they also want to put one of those electric dog collars around your neck so you can't venture off too far. If they allow you to roam freely, going too far without any restrictions or limitations, they'll feel like you're leaving them behind. Don't let someone else turn your open sky into a ceiling. When people ask you to think outside the box, they are really telling you to get inside their box. It takes strong character to resist the influence of other people, especially your loved ones.

## Character Mind-Set

I've always believed character is defined by what you do when no one is looking. Character is also forged when family and friends are looking at you under a microscope. Many in the NFL or entertainment industry receive a lot of fame because of the bad things they do. The loud, outspoken players get a lot more media attention than the ones who simply high-five their teammates, walk back to the huddle, and act like they've been there and done that before.

When I started playing sports, my dad always instructed me to show my coach the same respect I showed him and that's what I've tried to do, from elementary school to the NFL. It didn't matter to me if I was an All-Star, All-Pro, All-American, or a Super Bowl champ. I was still the same "yes sir, no sir" guy. I never allowed the level of my success to change who I was as a person or player.

I've witnessed many of my teammates and many in other professions come from the bottom and progress their way to the top or transition from being a reserve player to becoming a starter. As a result, the fame and stardom just completely changed who they were as people. I've watched money from a new contract create such a large ego within a player that he could no longer be reached, not even by his coach, family members, close friends, pastor, or agent. I can picture some of my teammates, as rookies, patiently signing every fan's autograph after practice as they aligned on the fence only to later forget where they came from and run to the locker room after practice, ignoring their fans on the way in.

If every player, both young and old, would remind themselves that this game has been going on before they were born
and will continue to go on when they're dead and gone, everyone would enjoy a blessed career and never for a second think
they are bigger than the game. If they can figure this principle
out while they're still young and humble, they'll have a better
chance at not getting caught up in assorted "circus acts" that often accompany fame. This also relates to parenting, and it works
both ways. Don't let your son's or daughter's success change
who you are as a parent. If my son won the lottery tomorrow,
I would still be the same hardworking man, providing for my
family as I am today. Parents, don't allow money or success to
change the hierarchy or the chain of command in the relationships you have with your children. Confidence is like money: It's
hard to gain and easy to lose. So is respect. Don't believe me?
I still vacuum my own floors every day. I've been doing it my
whole life, and no amount of fame or fortune will cause me to
lose sight of who I am or where I come from.

## Untested

When I was eight years old, my mom and I were in a very popular southern department store called Belk. I was waiting around
as she tried on a few dresses and other items she had found on
the sales rack. Not sitting down and behaving like she asked
me to, I started running as fast as I could, weaving in and out

through the clothing racks. I accidentally got my foot tangled up on one of the dresses that was hanging too low from one of the racks. Trying my best to stay on my feet and avoid knocking down the entire rack, I took a dive to the floor. I quickly got back to my feet, so no one would realize what had happened and laugh at me. I noticed a very nice watch lying on the floor. Without hesitation, I picked the watch up, and I returned it to a store employee. No one asked me to do it. I didn't even wait to show my mom what I'd found. I just took it to the lady at the cash register. I really saw no alternative.

It may seem like a small moment in the big scheme of things, but I still remember that as a defining moment in knowing who I was as a person. It was defining, because I passed a test. You don't truly know how strong you are until you are put into a testing situation. A. W. Tozer said, "God never uses anyone greatly until He tests them deeply." And five-time Super Bowl Champion Head Coach Bill Belichick said, "Talent sets the floor, but character sets the ceiling."

I've seen it happen so many times with guys who come into the locker room and are just waiting to get their paws on a big new contract. Once they do, they become a whole different person. I've witnessed athletes completely shut it down once they recieved the big pay day they were in pursuit of. That's a character issue. Reputation is what someone gives you, but character is who you are. As they say, it takes character to keep your eyes on where you're going. So, keep your focus.

## Tell the Truth

I have a hard time telling the truth when it means I might hurt someone's feelings. How about you? But, when I'm not truthful, the situation ends up coming back to bite me in the butt. Telling the hard truth is another positive lesson I've learned from my wife. She's a firm believer in giving the other person the decision about how to respond to the truth. When we hold back, we take away someone's right to deal with the truth, and, in effect, we're lying to them.

Sounds like a recipe for disaster, right? We can't help others, even our loved ones, if we aren't being honest with ourselves and sharing our truth in a loving way. People will treat you the same way you treat them. If you're not honest, you'll become angry and resentful—and the same will be true for those around you.

You want to know the truth, right? I believe in treating people the way that you want to be treated. If you don't genuinely love yourself and you're not completely happy with who you are and where you are in life, it will be extremely hard for you to love others. Part of the truth is that you have a dream. I read somewhere that a dream is simply a promise your heart makes to you while you're asleep. You don't want to forget where you came from, but you don't want to stay where you are either. You have a decision to make: Continue to live in the past and lose the ball before you cross the goal line, or hold on tight to your dreams and score the winning touchdown. So, which is it going to be?

# Where You're Going
# with Your Money

In the early stages of my professional career, my college sweet-heart and soon-to-be-wife of my dreams, Linda, and her sister Jasmely, thought I was cheap with my money. I would visit Linda and her family in Miami, and we'd do the normal boyfriend and girlfriend stuff like go out to dinner, catch a movie, shop, and walk around the mall.

At times, she and her sister thought my visits to Miami should've been a bit more extravagant or I should've been more willing to pay the food bill when we'd all eat out. As we got to know each other better, they better understood me and my views toward money—and that I didn't want money to be the focus of any relationship I was involved in. They also respected the fact that I was responsible for a lot more than myself. The experience did help me find my true definition of "cheap." I mean, at the end of the day, who wants to be known as being cheap?

My dictionary gave one definition of cheap as being low in price, so I found it very difficult to label myself as being cheap, because I liked and had nice things. I also had all the things I desired to have. So, their comments confused me more than they angered me, if you know what I mean. And, as fate would have it, my sister-in-law, Jasmely, ended up marrying someone more frugal than I am.

I've always been the type of person who's not easily persuaded or influenced by others. As early as the 5th grade, I lived by the mantra, "Peer pressure is overrated," and I truly believed that. As I've gotten older, and have been through many experiences on different teams, I've adopted a new slogan, "Run your own race." In sports and in life, so many of us don't run our own race, because we're getting pressured and influenced by our surroundings. This causes us to do things just because someone else is doing them. I quickly witnessed how fast a person could find themselves in a jacked-up situation from trying to be someone they weren't or from doing something they were never meant to do.

When it comes to your money, I strongly advise you to run your own race. Trust me when I say, "You won't have much help earning it, but you'll have plenty of help spending it." It's not about keeping up with the Jones' or pleasing anyone else. It's about making sound decisions that help get you closer to *your* goals in life.

The Bible poses the question, "Who starts building a house and does not count the full cost?" For us, this means we need to count the full cost of our finances, time, investments, decisions, and relationships. Most of all, we should count the cost of any idea that isn't ours but might have an impact on our goals. I've been accused of forgetting where I came from—and yes, that hurts—but I've never been accused of being a person who doesn't know where I'm going. Can the same be said about you?

## TURNOVERS

- We waste our time and energy blessing people with unhealthy mind-sets. The superficial blessings we gift them will never be appreciated or make them truly happy, because their mind-sets haven't been altered.

- We are setting ourselves up for failure when we get too complacent and comfortable inside our boxes and stop wanting more—or we make the mistake of allowing someone else to convince us to try their box on for size.

- Parents allow the hierarchy or the relationship between them and their children to change based on their child's success and money. When this happens, a level of respect from the child toward their parents is lost.

## TAKEAWAYS

- Score more touchdowns than touchbacks in your life. Be an asset and not a liability.

- Know the company you keep. Keep the squares out of your circle. The same people who celebrate your success and exalt you will be the same people who celebrate your failure and drop you.

- Relationships are a lot like investments. Some pay off and others you lose big on.

# Chapter 13

# SPIRIT VERSUS FLESH

We're all born into a problem. As a result, we're in constant warfare. Not only are we born into a battle, we're each drawn into our own individual battles. I expressed in an earlier chapter how everything we go through and every obstacle we face in life all starts and ends with our minds. Mind over matter, remember? This is why it's so important for us to properly train our minds, because our bodies will automatically follow whatever our minds instruct them to do. When we make decisions based on our faith in God, we may still fall, but we will always fall forward. In other words, if our decisions are incorrect and they take us down the wrong paths in life, we will eventually end up where God meant for us to be. The journey may take us a little longer, but just know that it was all a part of God's plan for our lives. The process must be realized before it's revealed to us. On the contrary, when we make our decisions based on fear, we always fall backwards, because God didn't give us the spirit of fear. And we will not only go down the wrong paths in life, we also will never reach the final destination God designed for us.

As Coach Mickey Andrews used to share with us as it relates to falling, "It's okay to fall as long as you're on your way up before you hit the ground." Life is made up of daily warfare between the flesh and the spirit. We must make intentional decisions whether to be obedient to God and listen to our hearts. Or, we can follow the flesh and be pulled away by our emotions, earthly temptations, and unhealthy people. Unfortunately, there's no film to watch or game plan to study to help prepare you for the battle of life. The enemy comes at us in many forms and from all angles. Therefore, it's critical for us to stay ready, so we don't have to get ready.

For someone to get a reaction out of another person, that person must first value their opinion. It's not difficult to dismiss thoughts and emotions when they're triggered by strangers or someone you don't care about. But when attacks come from the people we love, like our parents, siblings, best friend, or trusted advisor, how do we respond? How can we foresee things of this nature happening? I've been faced with these types of situations on many occasions throughout most of my adult life. I'll be the first to tell you that they don't get any easier, and they don't stop recurring.

# Is Everything Spiritual?

There are battles we wage that range from annoying to life-threatening. But, at the root, it's always a spiritual battle. The origins of the challenges we all face can always be traced back to someone making choices to either follow their flesh or follow their spirit. Persecution is certain. Our value to the kingdom, which is on display to the rest of the world, is a threat to the enemy. So why not focus on the real cause and, more importantly, the real solution? A great friend of mine, John Mason, often reminds me to "fight the issue and not the person."

The Bible says in Ephesians 6:12, "We do not wrestle against flesh and blood, but against principalities, against powers, against the rulers of the darkness of this age, against spiritual hosts of wickedness in the heavenly places." When you view life from this perspective, you won't take things personally. When someone offends you, instead of jumping into battle with that person, you can pause and choose the right response. I'll admit, this is very hard to do. However, I've pledged to myself to do a better job at responding to a situation instead of always reacting to it.

Playing defensive back my entire career programmed me to react to happenings, so it's second nature to me. When you become great at reacting while playing a sport, you usually get paid well for it. Consequently, when you constantly react in your relationships, you end up being lonely because of burning all your bridges. When playing football, it took me countless hours of hard work, practice, and preparation to become a professional. However, it will take that and much more for me to master responding instead of reacting when life happens to me. But one of the most valuable principles I've learned over my many years of playing sports is that practice and preparation are worth their weight in gold.

So, again, I ask is everything spiritual? Yes, all the time. We simply need our spiritual eyes to see it. The game is called Life and it lasts twenty-four hours a day, 365 days a year. Unfortunately, when we sign up for this game we don't get any days off and there's no off-season. Life can, at times, get the best of us all—especially when the daily battles start to pile up. Sadly, in life, we can't go around everything. Some things we must go straight through. Fortunately, what we go through can't compare to what God has for us on the other side. We must make an intentional decision to walk in the light or give in to the darkness. And to always remember that it's not over until you win.

Jesus said if we are faithful in small matters, we will rule over bigger ones. Every time we pass a faith test, God gives us a little more growth. He trusts us a little more, so He enlarges our territory. Every time we make the wrong decision, we stay in the same spot and miss an opportunity to be an example to those around us. We must understand the value of the investment God has put on our lives. As a result, we can stop adding value or investing into our portfolio of poor choices.

As parents, and as children, we should understand the struggle is bigger than us. When you are blessed, you can expect the enemy to come in and try to steal it. Sometimes, this takes on the form of jealousy and strife from those that rest right beside us. Don't take it personally. If you do, you're taking the bait. Remember, we're all fighting battles. With that said, first we must learn about our opponents. I'm a firm believer that knowing your opponent gives you the best chance of defeating them.

## Everyone Is in a Battle

When you understand that each one of us is in a battle between spirit and flesh—between good and evil, between peace and chaos—we can begin to give people more grace. Do you handle every situation perfectly? Do you sometimes react poorly? If you're like me, at times you may find yourself making permanent decisions in temporary situations. However, we all want grace and understanding. We can stop squandering our futures, if we stop trying to satisfy our short-term pleasures.

If we act and react out of emotion, we're destined to develop habits that keep this cycle going. It's only when we break the cycle, that victory and peace are possible. This means owning up to your role in the strife, following God's Word, and following your conscience. Sometimes, your role in the relationship of strife is simply the wrong mind-set. We develop what Bishop Walker calls the "Messianic complex" where we feel like we are another person's savior.

We often pray for God to fix an ongoing situation. He can take us out of the situation, but if we jump right back into the same situation, we are perpetuating the cycle. Stop harboring a fugitive. We aren't giving up on that person, we're releasing them into their destiny.

## Boundaries and Battles

It's natural for a child to want to help their parents or try to fix their parents' relationship. No child wants to see their parents get a divorce. Even as an adult, we sometimes cross the line into fighting other people's battles. I'm guilty as charged on both accounts. No marriage is perfect, but the only marriage you are responsible for is your own. When I experienced some financial success, I often tried to fix other people's relationships with money. Now, when I find myself in a similar situation, I stop and ask myself, *Is this my battle to fight?*

Why do we jump into other people's battles? Most of the time, we are slowly drawn over the line and don't realize what we're doing isn't normal or healthy. Sometimes, we become so used to dysfunction and fighting that the concept of peace seems impossible. So, we stay in other people's battles. Dysfunction becomes our new normal, and we assume everyone else is going through the same hell we are.

Most of the battles we face are due to not having good

boundaries. Boundaries are clear lines of responsibility in relationships. Again, we can only set these boundaries for ourselves. And it's up to other people to set their own. If you and your loved ones can sit down and communicate about boundaries, that's a bonus. Communication is very much like what I use to call prehab when playing football. Prehab sounds a lot like rehab, but prehab is done before there's an injury. Whereas, rehab is performed after an injury has occurred. I've experienced life long enough to understand that maintenance is a whole lot cheaper than repairs. Healthy boundaries will keep you away from many unnecessary battles. Can you imagine a sporting event with no rules? Of course not. Then, why are we so surprised when relationships become chaotic and hurtful when nothing is considered out of bounds?

Boundaries stop battles. But, more importantly, they prevent future battles from even starting. Boundaries also provide an answer to a situation before it arises. You can decide, in advance, how you will respond to any given situation in your life. And, just like with a game strategy, the more specific you are, the better the results.

My dad set some very clear boundaries with me early on: Respect your coach, do well in school, and don't act up in class. I knew there'd be consequences if I stepped out of bounds, so I avoided disrespecting my dad's rules. Most of the time, anyway. Because I knew what was out of bounds, I could stay inbounds. I encourage you to be ahead of the curve in every aspect of your life. Have the tough discussions now—the sooner the better. We must stop making excuses for other people's dysfunctions, while also learning not to engage in their dysfunctions. As one of my childhood preachers would often say before he dismissed us from church on Sundays, "The best business in the business is to mind your own business. If you don't have any business, make it your business to stay out of other folks' business, until you can find some business of your own."

## Respond Versus React

You have a choice in every situation. You can either respond or react. These two words begin with the same letter and sound like the same actions, but the difference between the two is enormous. And so are the results each one brings. Zig Ziglar said responding brings hope, production, and growth. It comes from a positive place and, in turn, breeds positive results. However, reacting comes from a place of anger, frustration, and other emotions, which breeds negative results.

Ships don't sink because of the amount of water *surrounding* them. Ships sink due to the amount of water getting *inside* of them. So, don't let what's happening around you get inside you and weigh you down. Some ships have also been known to sink because of who's on board. The Bible teaches us in Jonah 1:1-4 what can happen when we let someone like Jonah, who failed to respond to the commands of the Lord and reacted out of disobedience, occupy our boat. We have to stop holding onto people and things that weigh us down. When we let people or things—such as doubt, fear, guilt, resentment, and worry—occupy space in our residence, it forces us to put up a "no vacancy" sign in the windows of our souls. Then, we have no more room for all the good stuff like creativity, joy, love, peace, and patience to fill our spirits. So, be careful who you allow on your boat. And remember, you always have a choice.

## Motivation for Battle

It's amazing how much discipline and self-control I had when dealing with my coaches. This was something I learned how to do. And part of the motivation was the fact that football was the path to my goals. It was my way to make change. It was my ticket to the big show and, eventually, my job. But, I must admit, for many years I was very disciplined about relationships with my coaches and teammates. However, I didn't have the same patience or tolerance for some family and friends, whom I loved.

Sometimes I'd wonder: *How can I be so respectful, patient, and forgiving toward some of my coaches and teammates, when they don't always deserve my respect, and then be disrespectful, impatient, and unforgiving to my parents, siblings, and other loved ones? How can I be so patient and loving with my children when I'm so impatient with my wife?*

When we ask ourselves questions like these, we are really asking about motivation, which is part of our character. Was it because I was chasing after a big check and didn't want to risk it by having a bad attitude? Was I afraid I'd be released or cut by the team? In life, whatever you want more of, you give more of. If you want more peace, if you want continued success, then ask yourself what you're doing to obtain it—and ask why. Sure, you can make assumptions about the motivations of others. But you'll never truly know what's in their hearts. Instead, focus on your own character, motivations, and boundaries. Wholeheartedly understand your own why and be conscious of your authentic intentions. As stated in Matthew 6:21, "For where your treasure is, there will be your heart also."

## Relationships Can Change

Right now, my kids are dependent on me and listen to what my wife and I have to say, *most* of the time. That's because they respect us as their parents. If they grow up and become more financially successful then my wife and me, would we ever reverse roles? Of course not. If parents allow this to happen, I feel some level of respect will go out of the window as well. I have witnessed parent-child relationships reverse roles to the point where the child is telling their parents what they can and can't do, or they are telling them to take a seat as if they were disciplining their own parents. From the outside looking in, people can't tell, or don't know, if they are friends, siblings, or which one of them is the parent.

How does this happen? How do we arrive here? Why do parents of successful individuals stop being responsible parents? Why even reverse the roles? My theory is based on this "golden" rule: Whoever has the gold is the king and makes the rules. But this only happens in families when money attacks unhealthy boundaries. When this happens, confusion and war break out.

If money has changed a relationship you're involved in, try to respond according to the spirit, rather than reacting according to the flesh. To maintain healthy relationships, it's important to have clear boundaries, to always be respectful, and to always forgive. Before allowing money to change the hierarchy and dynamics in your relationship with your child (or loved one), decide which one of the two you want the most: Your relationship with this person or their money.

## Choose to Respond with the Spirit

We all meet people with preexisting issues, dysfunctions, and fallacies that have nothing to do with the other person, but they have a great effect on the relationship the two of you are trying to build. You can't always judge a person by the chapter of life you meet them in. Yes, you may have been taken advantage of or mistreated in the past, but don't join the haters. Don't close your heart to opportunities that can be a blessing.

We must get to the point where we only listen to, and focus on, what God is doing for us, instead of focusing on what everyone else has already done to us. As a result, we'll realize what God is doing in our lives is tied to our destinies, while realizing that what everyone else has already done to us is tied to a lie. There are no losses in life, only lessons. You only fail at something when you don't learn anything from it. As long as you learn something, the lesson can transform your failure into a learning experience. So, learn the lesson and move forward with clearer boundaries.

In the sports world, if a reporter writes something bad about you and then wants to interview you again about something else, respond, but don't react in the flesh. Coaches demand the best out of you, and sometimes they cuss and scream, but you can choose how to respond to them. I've always responded with a "yes sir" or "no sir" and then reacted with how I play on the field. In any situation, pause and try to put yourself in the other person's shoes. Try to understand how they feel or what they may be thinking. Then respond with the spirit.

James 1:19 says, "Be swift to hear, slow to speak, and slow to wrath." This verse explains why we're all born with two ears and one mouth. And yes, this is a battle between flesh and spirit. On our own, we all react based on emotion. But with God's help, we can respond with the spirit and see peace grow.

# TURNOVERS

- When we take attacks on our lives as personal, we attempt to fight back with our flesh.

- When we feel like we are being singled out and we are the only ones going through constant warfare and attacks, the frustration can cause us to make permanent decisions in temporary situations.

- We often react to life when it happens to us, instead of responding to it. As result, we burn a lot of bridges out of anger, and we build even more barriers to protect ourselves. An overcautious person burns the bridges of opportunity before he gets to them.

# TAKEAWAYS

- Remember to fight the issue and not the person. All battles we are faced with in life are spiritual battles. You can't win a spiritual war fighting with your flesh.

- Poor choices result in rich consequences. Bill Cowher, the head football coach for the Pittsburgh Steelers when I played for them, would always say, "We control our choices and decisions until we make them. Then, they controlled us." When faced with a challenging situation, be sure you call a time-out and think before you respond or react.

- Before allowing money and power to alter a relationship with a loved one or friend, decide which one you want most.

# Chapter 14

# GUILT VERSUS GUILTLESS

After winning the Super Bowl in 2006, my four-year-long rookie contract with the Pittsburgh Steelers was completed, and I would become an unrestricted free agent the minute the clock struck midnight. Or, at least, that's what I thought would happen. If only things had gone that smoothly. What are the odds that the end of my free agent year would fall on the same year that the NFL's old Collective Bargaining Agreement (CBA) expired? After hours of back and forth negotiations and free agency being pushed back for a couple of weekends in a row, I finally signed a six-year contract with the Tennessee Titans. I felt like I'd just gone through the college recruiting experience and gotten drafted all in the same day. Sure, it was an emotional roller coaster and a very draining experience, but it was all worth it.

I didn't just have one of the best seasons statistically of my career. I also had one of the best seasons as a defensive back and defensive player within the entire league. In fact, my fifth year in the league (and first as a Titan) was so dominant there were lots of debates and discussions about me being one of the biggest snubbed players from the NFL Pro Bowl that season. Going into my sixth season, I started off red-hot again, not skipping a beat and still on fire from the previous season. However, I ended up hurting my neck pretty badly about three-quarters of the way through the season. As a result, I was placed on injured reserve, and I had to come to grips with the reality of not being selected as a Pro Bowl player for yet another season.

I was frustrated and disappointed. It was almost like God had just pushed the pause button on my life. I was starting to doubt and beginning to lose hope on being able to accomplish a dream of mine for the first time in my life. However, God's pause is not permanent. His pause didn't mean it was over for me. No matter how bad it seemed, He kept me alive while He had me on pause. Now that I think about it, there is no such thing as a neck injury that is *not* bad.

I've always been a hard hitter and a very aggressive play-er. Over time, the hitting took its toll on my body, particularly my neck. In year six, I made a tackle in a game against the Cincinnati Bengals, and, in an instant, I was covered in a pile of players. One of my own teammates dove head first into the pile and hit me helmet-to-helmet. The impact triggered a spinal cord seizure, which made my lower body shake uncontrollably. From the stories I've been told by my teammates, I'm sure glad I didn't witness the event myself. Lying there on the field, I didn't know what was going on. I'm usually more courageous and stubborn than I am afraid, so I said to myself, *I'm walking off this field. No matter what!*

The medics and coaches told me not to move. Even after the seizure went away, they kept telling me not to move. "I'm all right," I insisted. There was no way I was going to allow them to carry me off that field. I had to get up and walk off by myself, because my parents, siblings, and family were all watching, including all my little cousins who thought of me as a superhero. Besides, I prayed before every game, "Lord, let me walk off this field the same way I walked on. I don't care if I'm limping, but at least I'll be walking."

So, after ten to fifteen minutes, I got up, little by little, and walked off very slowly. The guys on my team were really shaken up over what they'd witnessed. That's because up until this incident, I looked pretty much indestructible. And so did our team. But, we lost that game, and my teammates lost me for the rest of the season. One of my closest friends in the league and teammate at the time, David Thornton, wouldn't leave my side as I hopelessly lay there, even when the refs demanded that he move. Determined, he remained and continued to pray. That evening, sitting beside each other on the long and painful plane ride home, I told him how much that meant to me. I was a lot more scared then I realized at the time, and his prayers and his presence gave me the extra love and motivation that I needed.

His response brought tears to my eyes. "C'mon bruh, we are truly family. Brothers on the field, brothers off the field, but more importantly brothers in Christ. I wasn't leaving your side until you got up and told me you were good. What we have is far deeper than this game of football. God strategically put us in each other's lives for not only a reason and a season, but for a lifetime. We might not have known each other from the womb, but we will definitely be a part of each other's life until the tomb."

My best friend who lives back in my hometown in South Carolina later told me he was watching the game on live TV. He saw the hit and thoroughly examined the replay to see if he could see what had happened to me, but as my body started to shake uncontrollably, the network abruptly changed the picture. The next thing he knew his phone rang, and it was my number calling. He was almost too afraid to answer, but, when he did, it was my voice. Depending on what day of the week it is and whether or not my friend wants to be honest, he'll tell you my voice scared the life out of him. I missed the last five games of the season to have surgery. I went on to play the next season, but I was weaker. And also stronger.

## Weakness and Strength

The Bible says in 2 Corinthians 12:10, "When I am weak, then I am strong." What a ridiculous statement, right? When I woke up from the surgery, the doctor said he had never seen bone as strong as mine. That was one of the advantages of me working out all the time. I was taught that being strong helps prevent injuries. When I dislocated my shoulder, they put it back in place, and I played like it never happened. I never had surgery to repair it and never missed a game.

As we were leaving the hospital, the surgeon told Linda to make sure I didn't go to the gym the next day. But a couple of days later, I was there. Even though I was weak, I was determined to stay strong and to quickly regain my strength. The following season, my best friend, Lavar, who has never missed a game, asked me why I consistently tugged on my right glove after every play during the game. At the time, I was too ashamed to share my truth with him. So, I didn't tell him the truth until after I retired. The truth was, every time after contact, my entire right arm would go numb, and it would go all the way down into my hand and fingers—and still does to this day. To try and quickly regain feeling before the next snap, I created the habit of pulling up my glove tighter and firmer, to make it fit extra snug on my hand.

I ended up playing six more years after that surgery. Some guys hurt their necks like I did and never play again, so I was thankful. It took a lot of mental toughness to continue playing, but my weakness made me a stronger player. In life, you don't always get what you want. In life, you get what you are. I was committed to my commitment.

## Pro Bowl

The next season, which happened to be my seventh year in the NFL, I went to the Pro Bowl. In so many ways, I wasn't even half the man I was the year before or in previous years throughout my career. The injury changed me, and it changed the way I played the game. I had to play smarter and try not to use my head every time I tackled.

My brother once told me that since my surgery I looked a little gun shy. I quickly asked him if he had ever hurt his neck—and if so, could he offer me any advice about playing in the NFL with an injured spine. That was a short conversation.

God showed me through the experience of being injured, and the long recovery that followed, that it's never been about me. *Chris Hope, I can use you however and whenever I want to use you. It's never been about you.* 2 Corinthians 12:9, "But he said to me, 'My grace is sufficient for you, for my power is made perfect in weakness.'" The moral of that scripture is: less of me and more of Him.

## Saved by the Reaper

After going through 12 NFL training camps, in my opinion, the most dreadful days of camp had nothing to do with the scorching summer heat or the long, fully padded, physical, two-and-a-half-hour, two-a-day practices. Coaches like to refer to these days as the "dog days" of camp when everyone, including them, wants to go home. The most gloomy, grim, hated, horrible, and painful days of training camp actually came when camp was coming to its end. Some like to refer to it as "good old doomsday" when the team's roster has to be trimmed down to fifty-three players, leaving around 1,100 players without a job.

Time and time again, I've watched so many of my teammates and closest friends get the "undesirable" tap on the shoulder from one of the members of the team's front office, referred to as a scout. We used to call him the Grim Reaper. The Grim Reaper would have the unenviable task of telling them that their dreams of playing in the NFL for this respective team had come to an end.

It was a Saturday morning, and it was our first fully padded practice in front of our fans. Detroit was still rather new to me, but I was beginning to get settled in. It was an entirely different city to me, so I had to learn a different route to work. I had different teammates, different coaches, different trainers, a different locker room, different cafeteria, different cooks, and a different jersey number—but the game of football never changes. The game and the field were my sanctuary. They gave me peace and brought me calmness. They were the only things I was familiar with. They were the only reason I was there.

We started practice off with a high-intensity and very physical team drill called "team run" in which our offense would be practicing some of their regularly called "run plays" to get their timing right. We, as a defense, were trying to begin to establish an identity of toughness by executing some of our stout and dominating run defenses to prevent a team from running the ball down our throats all game.

I was in at strong safety, and my new coaches wanted to see what the old man had left in his tank. So, they called a safety blitz off the right side of our defense. What a perfect call to set the tone of practice with. I wisely walked back and forth to the end of the line of scrimmage, playing mind games with the quarterback, as he scanned our defense trying to see what defense we were in. I looked him right in the eye and basically dared him to snap the football. He tried to call my bluff, but I kept my poker face on. Just like a wise veteran, I easily tricked our quarterback and timed my blitz off the edge up perfectly. He didn't recognize the blitz, however. As a result, he failed to shift the offensive line to my side to count me in their blitz protection. Consequently, I burst off the corner into the backfield untouched and exploded into the running back for about a five-yard loss. Everyone went crazy on our defense, and our coaches all started chest-bumping and high-fiving one another. After that big collision and all the celebrating, I felt a little different, but, like always I knew, sooner or later I would shake it off.

We went on to the next drill, and I went on having my best day at camp so far. The next period of practice, a running back burst through a gigantic hole on our defense, appearing to have what looked like a nice gain of yardage. Then, in a blink of an eye, I came up from my safety position, out of nowhere, and I put him right on his sit bone. It was like I took the breath from the fans, just as they were about to start cheering for the offense. Although I knew I would have to deal with pain later, I was in a zone. I was getting comfortable with the new defense, and I was starting to feel like myself. A few plays later, I read the eyes of the quarterback, and I cut off a receiver coming across the field on an over-route and picked off the pass and returned it for a big gain. To say I had a great day, would be an understatement. It finally started to feel good to do what I came to Detroit to do. However, that would be short lived.

After practice, my neck was stiffer than a dead man's frozen shadow. It never loosened up after the first big hit, but, like always, I just blocked it out and pushed through it. I couldn't wait to get undressed. I ran off the field into the locker room. There's nothing that some good old-fashioned prehab treatment—a couple of aspirin, a cold tub, and a hot tub—can't fix. I basically drowned myself in the cold tub for about 15 minutes and then did the same in the hot tub. Neither one worked. I figured some long prayer once I got back to the room and a good night's rest would do the trick. Boy, was I wrong.

Ever since that day, my neck never was the same, and I spent the rest of my time in training camp in extreme pain, unable to sleep. I'm not exaggerating when I say I didn't sleep. I didn't even get a little bit of rest, because I just couldn't get comfortable. My neck was hurting, and the pain started radiating down my right arm into my right hand. And my mind started racing: *Why am I here? Is it even worth it? What else do I need to prove? What will the people say if I quit? I can't quit now. I'm too close. I have to properly pass the torch over to the next generation of talent from my hometown: Stephon Gilmore, Jadeveon Clowney, and Cordarrelle Patterson. Man, I miss my family.*

My daughter Crislyn was about seven months old. Before I left for camp, she and I had built the strongest bond ever. I missed her touch, her smell, her smile, and her little giggle. And to see her on FaceTime every morning just broke my heart. I never told a soul how I was feeling at the time. Not my wife, not any of the trainers, not a one of my coaches or my newly made friends. I just toughed it out like I always did. I just kept my head down and never quit. Quitting had never been an option for me, so I wasn't going to start now. I had to finish my race no matter what it looked like at the end. The real question was, "Would I rust or wear out first?" That was an easy answer for me. I was going to finish what I started, even if killed me.

If I quit, I would be quitting on more than myself. I would be quitting on my family, my daughter, my parents, my siblings, my community, the people who looked up to me, and, most importantly, one of my great friends and my defensive back coach, Marcus Robertson, who was responsible for bringing me to Detroit. Every night I prayed to God as I lay in bed with all the lights out and my eyes wide open for Him to give me a sign on what to do.

Every day I fought a constant battle inside my mind. Every morning I would FaceTime with Linda and Crislyn and go to practice like everything was all good. I started noticing that my speed, explosiveness, power, and quickness weren't like they normally were. My ability to effortlessly avoid blockers, burst to the football, and make plays on the ball carrier didn't seem as natural anymore. The nerve pain from my neck was starting to travel to my lower back and down into my hamstrings, which affected my legs. That's when the game changed for me. I've never wanted to quit something so badly in my life, but I just couldn't do it. I was still waiting on my sign from God.

Then, one morning at breakfast, I was thumbing through my phone as I begin to put jelly on my toast, and I came across a quote from the Dalai Lama who'd been asked what surprised him the most about humanity. He said, "Man sacrifices his health in order to make money. Then he sacrifices money to recuperate his health. And then he is so anxious about the future that he does not enjoy the present; the result being that he does not live in the present or the future; he lives as if he is never going to die, and then dies having never really lived." I almost started crying right there in front of my teammates who were sitting at the table eating breakfast with me. God spoke directly to me through that quote, and, in that moment, I asked Him to save me from myself.

And He totally did. I kid you not. We had a team meeting right after breakfast. After our meeting, we were to get dressed for our early morning practice. As I walked out of the meeting, all of a sudden, I felt so relieved. As the crowd dispersed to the locker room to get dressed for practice and all the noise died down in the hallway, the good old Grim Reaper touched my shoulder. When he touched me, at first, I was shocked, but I quickly turned to him and said "Wow! God sent you? Thank you!" The Reaper is the last person a player wants to see, but I completely welcomed him.

"It's okay. You don't have to be nervous. Trust me, it's okay!" I told him. His words to me were, "This is the toughest thing I've ever had to do in my career this far. I went to FSU, so I've watched you play for years, and I've always been a big fan of yours. You're amazing player, awesome leader, the perfect teammate, and an even better person. These guys look up to you and love being around you. We will definitely miss having you around." I was humbled and motivated by his kind words, but my spirit was as free as it's ever been. So, the man I watched my teammates duck and dodge for years was a person that I couldn't wait to meet. Finally, getting that touch from the Reaper wasn't so bad after all. If he hadn't come for me, who else was going to save me from me?

## Survivor's Remorse

I don't question why God chooses to use me anymore, but I'm very grateful and honored that He does. But, to be honest, sometimes I do feel guilty. For example, in church, when the preacher asks, "Does your praise match or reflect what God has blessed you with? If God's been good to you, clap and make some noise." I sometimes want to shout and do backflips. But, then I fear my thankfulness will be mistaken for pride. Almost like I'm rubbing my success in other people's faces. I mean, how do I justify driving a $300,000 car, when others are walking? How do I explain living in a 10,000+ square-foot home when others have no place to stay? How can I throw more food away in one day than some people are able to consume in an entire week? How do I enjoy a hopeful outlook on the future, when others believe their best days are behind them?

One of my biggest "guilts" in life is the fact I've had the opportunity to live out my childhood dream and make a great living for myself and my family by being able to run, jump, kick, fall down, tackle people, and catch a football. Whereas, one of my little cousins has never had the opportunity to do any of these activities, because she is paralyzed from the waist down from a car accident that she got into after coming to watch me play a college football game. While I've traveled the world freely, she's been permanently married to her wheelchair since that day.

We aren't defined by what we go through in life, but rather how we come out of it. My cousin has truly been an inspiration to me, and she gave me the strength to keep fighting when times became difficult in my life. Even from a young age, she never allowed that accident to stop her from where she was going. She was crowned homecoming queen during her senior year in high school and then headed to Coastal Carolina for college. She didn't let what happened turn her into a victim. Instead, she allowed it to transform her into a visionary.

You see, enabling is a habit. A bad one, I might add. It's not good for the person who is doing the enabling or the person who is allowing it to happen. Not only did my cousin not allow us to enable her, she also didn't complain about her situation or throw herself a pity party. Zig Ziglar says, "The problem with pity parties is that very few people come, and those who do, don't bring presents." My cousin maintained a positive attitude and a winning mind-set.

How you perceive something will determine your perspective about it. When we understand how powerful our thoughts and words are, we will think before we speak and think about what we say. Allow your words to justify you and not condemn you. I honestly learned this lesson from my little cousin. Because, for a long time, I told myself that I was to blame for what happened to her. We must all learn to talk ourselves "to life" rather than talk ourselves "to death."

Guilt. That's a serious problem I have. How about you? OK, some of you may be thinking, "Must be nice to have that problem, Chris." Okay, let's talk about that. People with this type of attitude are always looking for a handout. Should I have not aimed so high or worked so hard? Do other people's negative choices mean that my positive choices should be torn down? Do I have to suppress or downplay how good God has been to me so that I won't offend those around me? If I blow my candle out, it will not make your candle shine any brighter. Don't allow people to minimize your greatness and your life's calling just to help them to maximize their insecurities. Instead, I want to be an example of hard work and an example of God's grace and mercy.

How do you get to guiltless and simply appreciate what God has blessed you with? How do you celebrate all the hard work you've put in and not feel like you're going to offend someone? Survivors remorse isn't just the name of a recent television series produced by LeBron James—it's a real feeling. Successful people, particularly when they're from very poor communities, often feel remorseful, because "he's the one guy who made it out of the neighborhood," or "she's the one woman who had the chance to go to college and pursue a great career."

I believe my culture still has traces of ancient tribal rituals— where newborns are prayed over with the question, "Are you the one to save us?" By now, you know that I believe we're supposed to honor our mother and father and help those in need. But, we are not saviors. That's God's job! And He has already proved to us and provided for us by sending His only son Jesus to die on the cross for us.

## Guiltless

Let me be clear: Guilt is an unhealthy emotion. Guilt, along with any actions motivated by guilt, is just wrong—every time. Yes, we may feel convicted by God, but God does not place guilt on people. Instead, He gives humility, love, joy, and compassion. And those are the motivations to follow.

2 Corinthians 9:7 says, "So let each one give as he purposes in his heart, not grudgingly or of necessity; for God loves a cheerful giver." What this verse is saying is give from a grateful heart. Help people from a place of humility, but don't receive the curse of guilt from others, or from yourself. Parents, don't do things for your kids out of guilt. You don't *owe* anyone anything, but you can *choose* to give. The real blessing is that you have a choice.

Romans 13:8 makes this pretty clear. "Owe no one anything except to love one another, for he who loves another has fulfilled the law." How much has the lie of guilt cost you? It has cost me more than I care to count—in time *and* money. What are you spending every day based on guilt? Guilt is a debt you can never pay off. Are you ready to let yours go?

## TURNOVERS

- When we make ourselves feel guilty and blame ourselves for other people's lives, we become bashful and mute when telling others how good God has been to us, but we boldly share with the world through social media when things in our lives are on shaky ground.

- We make the mistake of trying to blow out our own candles, in hopes, that others around us will get to shine. Instead, we have to become comfortable in our own skin when making the transition from fitting in to standing out.

- When we try and take on the responsibility of being our families' and close friends' savior. That God's job. Guilt is a debt that we can never pay.

## TAKEAWAYS

- Learn how to be fruitful during your frustration and pray through your situation. Prayer is a significant time you can spend talking with God, so be intentional about what you pray for. It's the strength, not the length, of our prayers that matters. Make sure your family and friends are "praying" for you and not "preying" on you.

- When God chooses to use us, our testimonies and stories aren't just for us and our glory. They are for others

to learn from and be inspired by. It's never just about
you.

- Start talking yourself "to life" and stop talking yourself
  "to death." Allow your words to justify you, not condemn you.

# Chapter 15

# LIVING SOLO VERSUS BUILDING A TEAM

Probably the biggest parenting realization I've had since becoming a parent is this: My parents weren't so crazy after all. I can remember some of the things my mom and dad taught me when I was younger. At the time, I thought they were evil people who didn't want me to enjoy and experience life to its fullest. But now that my wife and I have our own children, the amount of stress parenting brings is just as overwhelming and gut-wrenching as a football game coming down to a game-winning field goal or a basketball game ending on a buzzer-beating shot from half-court. And the stress is unlike any other, because it's based on genuine, intense love and care.

Think about that when you communicate with your parents or decide you want to judge them. And think about the massive responsibility parents have *before* you decide to have a child of your own. Parenting is truly a trial and error type of experiment. You can prepare, plan, and read all the books you want about parenting, but you'll never truly understand the level of responsibility and commitment that comes along with parenting until you become a parent yourself. Matt Walsh explained it like this, "Parenting is the easiest thing in the world to have an opinion about, but the hardest thing in the world to do." Parents are not your enemies. Most are doing the best they can with the means they have and with the knowledge they have.

One of my biggest regrets is not having my kids when I was younger. I would have loved for my kids to have seen me play football and be at an age where they could understand what I was doing. I wish they could've had the experience of coming to watch me practice during training camp and to come run around and play on the field with me afterward. I wish they could have come down to the field on game day and into the locker room after games.

But, on the flip side, I also know I wouldn't have been as engaged as a parent as I am now. To be in your children's memories tomorrow, you have to be in their lives today. My commitment and focus on my career were so demanding, intense, and self-centered during that time, I know for a fact I would've been a great provider but a terrible father. I was all about me. I flew solo for much of my football career. Besides, money can't buy seeing their first steps and hearing their first words. There's nothing in this world I could have personally done myself, given to them, or done for them, to make up for those once-in-a-lifetime moments.

Every parent's goal is to create a better life for their children. Don't allow circumstances, conditions, or situations to change that. You want your child to be the best at whatever they choose to do, and you want to be able to afford that opportunity for them with no strings attached. As a parent, your only desire or expectation for your child is for them to love and respect you and others.

When you're a kid, everything is possible. You believe in magic. There are no limitations. The sky is like a canvas—you can paint things you like any way you want to and use any color you want or imagine. However, somewhere along the journey of growing up, reality sets in, and you start to focus more on what's practical and possible. But, kids like to focus more on what's impractical and impossible. That's what makes being a kid so great. Kids are born programmed to only know words or phrases like, "Yes, I can," "Let's do it," or "I can be anything I want to be when I grow up." We, as adults, or as parents, teach them words like, "No, don't do that," "You can't do that," or "Stop that, before you get hurt." Don't beat yourself up too badly—you're not alone. We, as parents, are all guilty of this in one way or another.

One of our most important roles as parents is to keep a childlike faith alive in our kids. Try to find a balance between teaching your kids what's possible and not possible, while avoiding putting them in a box. Being too positive can be just as dangerous as being too negative. Just be realistic with them. Allow them to color outsides the lines and encourage them to never put the keys to their happiness in someone else's hands.

I learned a pretty impressive lesson from my witty four-year-old daughter, Crislyn, when I began to coach her about the "importance" of staying inside the lines when coloring. As she began to scribble uncontrollably all over the piece of construction paper I gave her and started to color outside the lines, or boundaries, of the page and onto the kitchen table, I quickly stopped her and explained that when she colors, the objective is to stay *inside* the lines. Lord knows she's my child. Because she told me, "Coloring outside the lines doesn't mean that I can't color good, Daddy. It just means that the piece of paper you gave me to color on is too small." Impressive, right? I know. I didn't have a response either.

## Building a Team

When you're building a team, it's very important that the people on your team all share the same goal. They don't necessarily have to see everything the same way; however, having the same end goal is very important to being able to work together to accomplish what you're pursuing. If you don't have the same end goal, you can end up being wounded, hurt, or held back by those very same people on your team and by those you're trying to help.

The hardest part of success isn't achieving it—it's *maintaining* it. You don't only want your team to hear what you're saying, you also need them to *see* what you're saying. You need them to understand your perspective. You see what I'm saying?

How or what you see helps determine your destiny. If you, or those around you, don't see anything, you'll always end up chasing everything. But, if you can see it, you'll be able to say it. And, when you can start saying it, that's when you'll be able to seize it.

Part of nurturing faith in your children involves not letting your "grown-up" reality pour into their minds and hearts. Yes, as they grow older, children need to understand how the world operates. But, make sure you're sharing hope and not just disappointment. Every night as my wife and I pray over our children before they lie down to sleep, we always ask God to remind us to speak life and positivity into our children's lives.

Think about the parent who told their child they were ugly or told their child they would never amount to anything. Unfortunately, these types of parents are operating from their wounds. That kind of negativity stunts a child's growth and perpetuates generational poverty—mentally, financially, and spiritually. Some things these types of parents say include:

Why should you have a chance to go to college if I didn't?

I made good grades in school and was never rewarded, why should I celebrate your work?

My parents didn't support me or have the money to get me

involved in extracurricular activities. I had to figure it out on my own if I wanted to do something extra. So why should I make it so easy for you?

In Proverbs 18:21, King Solomon wrote, "Death and life are in the power of the tongue, and those who love it will eat its fruit." We have that power as parents. We must speak life to our children. We must be intentional on building them up and loving on them, so they'll be prepared for whatever the world throws at them. As parents, we all know from our own experiences that our kids will have their fair share of being kicked around and beaten up by this world. At the same time, kids must learn to receive discipline and correction, if they're going to succeed in life. Coach Patrick Murphy said, "Un-coachable kids become unemployable adults. Let your kids get used to someone being tough on them. It's life—get over it."

As a parent, your kids are your responsibility, because you brought them into this world. Kids, while you're young and living under your parents' roof, it's your responsibility to honor your parents. If the process of instilling responsibility is omitted by the parents, as a child grows older, he or she will become the world's responsibility. One of my biggest accomplishments and proudest facts about myself is that I've never embarrassed my family name. My grandparents, parents, aunts, uncles, cousins, and siblings have all done a great job of creating a well-respected name for our family, and I've done my best to not bring shame to it. That's one of the most important ways to honor your family, and it doesn't cost you one red cent. Will Rogers said, "It takes a lifetime to build a good reputation, but you can lose it in a minute."

## Preparing for Success as a Parent

As a parent, how are you preparing for your child's success? Just like a mother prepares for the birth of her baby, it's better to be overprepared than underprepared. We must make room for the things we pray for, because we are expecting them to happen. Parents pray for the best for their children, and children pray to become successful. In spite of that, we all still make the honest mistake of forgetting to pray for God to enlarge our territory, both mentally and physically, so we're ready and able to receive the increase.

God is not a "deadbeat" dad. He never births what He's not willing to take care of. If you do your part, because God will most certainly do His, don't be surprised when success happens—be prepared! Being prepared simply means knowing what you're going to do next. Don't be like a dog chasing a car. If a dog possessed the speed and ability to actually catch a car, what would he do with it once he caught it? Trust me, he doesn't know either.

When it comes to your role as the "coach" of your kids, prepare yourself for the role of guiding them into being successful. To do this, imagine how you will handle their success.

Think about how your child's success will affect or change your life. Will you fall into the trap of depending on your children, emotionally and financially? Or will you continue to be a strong and trusted guide?

I often picture myself speaking to a room full of parents and asking, "Whose son or daughter plays sports? Please stand up." Then, I'll ask some follow-up questions. If I could somehow get every single parent of every single athlete in one room, these are the questions I would ask them:

- How many of you are vicariously living through your child, secretly thinking about the opportunities you coulda, shoulda, woulda had back when you played?

- Who's depending on your child to earn a scholarship, so you won't have to pay tuition?

- Who goes to every one of your child's games, already envisioning them playing professionally and dreaming about the lifestyle you'll be living after he or she starts getting paid?

- How many of you know each and every one of your child's coaches' names, addresses, and phone numbers, but don't know your child's favorite subject in school or their math teacher's name?

- What's your motivation? Are you grooming them to financially support you? Or are you preparing them to be a success in all areas of life with no strings attached?

## Preparation and Pressure

I often argue with my colleagues about the difference between preparation and pressure. Hypothetically, if I have a son who plays football, and he so happens to be good, he should technically have an advantage, because I have some professional knowledge and wisdom to pass on to him. Part of me wonders if I would encourage, or force, him to play. But another part says, *If he wants to play, how am I going help him?* How do I know the difference? How can I separate the two? I'll confess that I don't know the answer to these questions. But I can say this with all confidence: If you're investing time, with love as the motivation, you'll stay on the right track.

I already have my daughter doing cone drills with a soccer ball—and she started when she was two years old. Am I a terrible father? She also loves playing basketball. From my own experience, I know by playing soccer she will develop good eye coordination and quick feet, which will transition over into her basketball game. I'm not coaching her to one day get a paycheck, and I'm definitely not living my life through her. I just want her to be great in everything she does. And it's also a great way to spend my "daddy day care" hours. I can't express to you how great a four-year-old sleeps after a good workout on the track and football field. I already mentioned how managing expectations isn't easy for any of us, so I'm eating my own cooking.

We all must find a balance—and keep adjusting that balance with our kids. Again, the exact balance is a mystery, but there is a key: joy. Do you see joy in your child when they participate in an activity? Yes, there's a difference in the demand of the training (which isn't fun at the time) versus the joy of the sport. When the joy isn't there, parents sometimes go to the extreme with their kids just because they played when they were kids—or always wanted to. Believe it or not, the parents who push their kids the most are often the same parents who have never even played a sport before. How ironic is that?

Remember, to make it in professional sports, or any top-level endeavor, being highly self-motivated, being overly determined, and being extremely passionate about what you are going after is a *must*. The goal is to develop, and respond to, genuine interest. It should be organic, not forced. For example, many times my daughter will say, "Let's go play soccer, Dad," or "Let's go run on the track," and she doesn't have to ask twice. I'm ready to go. I might have wanted to ask her two days ago, but I didn't want to force it. Of course, as kids get older, more structure and discipline become part of the equation. Joy, love, and passion should be there first. And then, we, as parents, should arrive next with our love and support.

## Be There

Many professional athletes, or successful people in general, have kids with more than one woman or have been married more than one time. They also have very demanding schedules with limited time. As a result, they aren't always present in their kids' homes, let alone in their lives. This, of course, makes it more difficult to pass along knowledge, wisdom, and love. I've not only seen talent wasted, but lives wasted, because fathers weren't around to invest in their kids and to help them hone their skills.

Every child has potential and dreams. But potential and dreams require work, persistence, and personal guidance to come to fruition. Jesse Jackson says, "Your children need your presence more than your presents." Myles Munroe, a Bahamian evangelist and ordained minister, once said, "The wealthiest place on the planet is not in the Far East where they have oil in the grounds. It's not in South Africa where they have diamond mines. The wealthiest place on the planet is the cemetery. Because there you will find dreams never pursued, books never written, songs never sung, sermons never delivered, businesses never erected, talents never nurtured, and skills never developed."

Kids need to see love in action. And that starts at home with mommy and daddy. My wife and I put each other first, even before our kids. Second to that, the only thing that matters to us is our two kids. We're not blind to the rest of our family, but our priorities are clear, and that decision brings us much clarity and peace.

## Investing in What Matters

Ever heard the expression, "Those kids come from money."?

I'd like to propose a much better statement: "Those kids come from money management." The same pressures that arise in the sports world are also present in the business world, just in a totally different dynamic. Children who are born into wealthy families often deal with intense pressure to succeed financially. These kids, more than likely, will only be judged by how much more money they can attribute to their families' estates. While people like myself have the stress of trying to become "first-generation rich" and obtain wealth, these privileged kids are swallowed up by the pressures of trying not to be the one who blow their families' fortunes. Previously, I shared an old saying, "The first generation makes the money, while the second generation maintains it, only for the third generation to come through and blow it." As I sit back and look at it from the outside, to be honest, I don't know which one bears more pressure—trying to be the first one to get it or trying not to be the first one to lose it.

Some parents automatically assume their children will follow in their footsteps, without even asking their kids what they want to do with their own lives. Many times, parents express this assumption by forcing or expecting their kids to go to the same college they attended and to major in the same subject. Or, they may pressure their kids to work in the same line of business as them and to marry rich, or at least find a mate in the same profession as them.

Believe it or not, I've heard many of my own teammates and friends toy with the idea of marrying, or at least mating with, another athlete with certain traits, hoping they can create their own perfect athlete. I wish I were pulling your leg, but it's all true. In wealthy families, the pressures and expectations parents put on their children have been deadly—literally. Suicides, drug addictions, alcoholism, and incarceration have played a major role in so many wealthy kids' lives, and it's so disappointing. Everyone always wonders and can't understand what would make a kid, who seems to have it all, act out in such a negative way. And it's all because they haven't had the opportunities to live their own lives and decide their own futures.

Learning about money is very important, but money isn't the ultimate goal in life. In many of our lives today, money ranks right below oxygen in terms of level of importance. But, unlike oxygen, we condition our minds and hearts to believe that we will one day run out of money. Too many financially successful parents are lonely in their later years. This is because wealth has created an impenetrable wall around them—literally and relationally.

As parents, we want to build relationships with our kids that last a lifetime, through all the seasons of life. To accomplish this, we need to be there for our kids in every early season of life. My wise mentors often tell me things like:

- Value your relationship with your family.
- Value your relationship with your kids.
- Spend as much time with them as you can, because

they'll be grown by tomorrow.

The days of parenting your kids may seem long, but the years are short.

## Speaking the Vision

"Hi, I'm Chris Hope, NFL All-Pro and Pro Bowl Safety." I've said those words hundreds of times. But, you might be surprised about the timing of these words. At the end of every workout, I'd look in the mirror and introduce myself as Chris Hope, NFL veteran, Pro Bowl, and All Pro Safety. Yes, this statement eventually became true, but I began saying it the day I was drafted into the National Football League.

A vision is a picture God gives you of His finished work. The picture will cause you to push through your reality and to focus on your possibility. Now that He has shown you a glimpse of it, start speaking it. Words are powerful. Imagine the power your words have on your life. And imagine the power your words have on the lives and hearts of your children.

## TURNOVERS

- When we try to live through our kids and force them to take advantage of the opportunities we had, didn't have, or missed out on growing up, we are placing them at a disadvantage.

- Being too involved in our kids' lives to the point we're making decisions for them about their future also puts our kids at a disadvantage. We make being a kid, or participating in a sport, a job for them, when it's supposed to be a learning experience to help develop them. The pressure we place on our kids results in a loss of passion and love for what we're forcing them to do.

- When making money and becoming successful is our main priority and ultimate goal in life, we forfeit valuable and unforgettable moments in our children's lives that money or gifts can't replace.

## TAKEAWAYS

- Our parents aren't our enemies. They genuinely want what's best for us. They want us to grow up and become successful people so we can add value to this world. In most cases, they have every intention to help create a better life for us than they had growing up.

- Find a healthy balance when assisting your kids. Try

your best to keep a childlike faith in your kids, but be realistic with them. Too much positivity is just as dangerous as too much negativity. Teach them how to ride the waves. And don't get too high with the highs or too low with the lows.

- Time is our most valuable asset. Abigail Van Buren says, "If you want your children to turn out well, spend twice as much time with them, and half as much money."

# Chapter 16

# TACKLING ADVERSITY

When I was playing football in Pittsburgh, we used to have an event called "Friday Night Lights" during training camp. We'd all load up on several buses and go to a local high school to hold a high-intensity, fully padded night practice, which is how the event got its name. It felt just like a good old Friday night high school football game. However, before we started with practice, Coach Cowher would set a timer and we'd all spread out along the fences to sign autographs, take photos, and spend a little time with the fans. It was quite an event, with thousands of high schoolers, parents, and faithful Steeler fans in attendance.

Because of the intensity of the crowd and that unforgettable Friday night high school football atmosphere, these special practices were almost like a real game. In spite of the large crowd, loud noises, and the bright lights, the schedule of practice was pretty much the same as usual. Well, let me take that back. It was business as usual *except* for how we finished the practice off. During "Friday Night Lights" we finished with a goal-line stand. The last few plays of the practice were four plays of full live scrimmage between our starting offense and our starting defense. Just thinking about it now gives my body chills and gets my blood boiling. The amount of money from bets between the offensive and defensive players on the sidelines was chump change compared to the amount of trash being talked between the offensive and defensive players on the field.

I'll always remember one play in particular. As I look back over my professional career, this is one of those plays I can look back on and say, "This moment helped introduce Chris Hope, aka Hammer, to the rest of the NFL." To no one's surprise in the stadium, Jerome Bettis got the football on the very first play. But, to my surprise, a hole in our defense opened up like Moses' parting of the Red Sea. Except, I was standing in his path. I once heard a man say that a turtle can't get ahead without first sticking his neck out. Apparently, this was my moment to be a turtle.

In case you don't know the play and you're wondering how my nightmare ended, "You of little faith, why are you so afraid?" Matthew (8:26). Jerome had ninety-one career touchdowns over thirteen NFL seasons, and I'm proud to say he didn't get to practice spiking the football after that collision. His nickname was "The Bus." He was used to making it past the goal line—practice or not. I guess I earned the right to be called "The Bus Stop" for at least that one play.

## Adversity Will Come

I didn't only do what I was told to do, but I did what I was trained to do. And, I did what I had to do. I went in and hit him—and stopped him. As the whistle blew, I can just remember everyone being so excited, chest bumping, and delivering high-fives. I tried to lift my arm in the air to join in on the excitement, but it wouldn't cooperate. That's when reality sunk in. I had a brief come-to-Jesus moment, and I realized what it felt like to literally be hit by The Bus.

My arm stayed like that for the rest of the season. I couldn't brush my teeth, put on deodorant, or turn on the radio in my truck. So, you can only imagine, trying to make a tackle was out of the question. But, like they say, "Where there is a will, there is a way." I simply had to adjust my tackling style. As an old Chinese Proverb states, "A wise man adapts himself to circumstances, as water shapes itself to the vessel that contains it." So, I'd tackle with my chest sometimes. Other times, I'd grab the ball carrier with my one good arm and slingshot them to the ground. I thank God that I was a solidly built guy who was powerful and strong enough to run right into the ball carrier and not have to wrap my arms around them to make the tackle.

I attended Jerome Bettis's Hall of Fame induction ceremony in Canton, Ohio. In his closing remarks, he made the statement of the Hall of Fame being the Bus's last and final stop, where all the other football gods rested. I beg to differ. Truth be told, I'm really the last one to truly stop The Bus. "The Bus stops here," I used to joke with him. But, he surely made me pay an extra fair for my ride. I may have won that small battle, but he definitely won the war. (By the way, Jerome is an awesome guy, and I'm proud to call him one of my big brothers and good friends.)

Believe it or not, I'd rather face Jerome Bettis one-on-one on the goal line again, instead of tackling some of the personal issues I've been through since then. Having said that, and as crazy as it sounds, they've all been worth it. Do I regret throwing my body into that tackle? No. In fact, most of my regrets come from chances I didn't take, confrontations I didn't face, and challenges I didn't finish. What I've found to be true is, it's better to look back on life and say, "Wow, I can't believe I did or tried that," than to look back and say, "I wish I would have tried to do that."

Romans 5:4 tells us that perseverance brings character, and character brings hope. The very act of persevering until you tackle adversity or achieve your goal makes you a better person. My Grandmother Chris used to always tell me when I was younger, "Opportunities come all the time, but they sure won't wait around for us. We let them pass us by, because they are dressed up as hard work. If you want something bad enough, you'll make a way. If you don't, you'll just make an excuse." I refuse to let anything, or anyone, make me miss my calling. The reason is simple. I just won't let someone else have that kind of power over me.

When I went to college, I had to block out all the drama going on back at home. I had to compartmentalize these issues to avoid allowing other people's issues to mess up my focus to the point of missing the NFL draft. I can't imagine how much I would've blamed, hated, and resented them for missing my destiny. And I'm glad I don't have to.

I don't even want to imagine how different my life might have been if, instead of reaching my professional goals, I had to go back home. Don't be ashamed or afraid to share your history with people. Your history is an important part of your destiny. If you can gain an understanding from your history, you can gain control of your future. God will take our past pains and turn them into a promise. He can turn our sad story into a success story, if we are willing to face our issues and do the work that's necessary to get through them. Take it from me: The end goal is worth the effort.

## New Challenges Are Good

So many wonder why successful people keep pursuing new dreams, even when their finances would allow them to step back and chill. The answer is pretty straightforward. Successful people aren't wired to chill or relax. They're designed to keep setting goals and work toward them. And this wiring isn't just for simple, routine goals like getting a promotion, traveling out of the country, or even getting out of debt. Don't get me wrong, these are great goals to set for yourself, but I'm also talking about setting goals and involving yourself with something so much bigger than you are that it will still exist when you're gone.

Our biggest and wildest dreams are still little things to God. Our dreams may be over our heads, but they are still under His feet. The bigger your dreams, the bigger God must show up in your life, because you won't be able to do it by yourself. We have to be brave enough to go after things beyond our reach. Anything less than this is not living, it's simply existing. As Stephen Hunt says, "If you're not living on the edge, you're taking up too much space."

That's why so many people struggle when they retire. The examples are endless. Maybe it's an actor struggling with not being able to act anymore, or a soldier who comes home wounded and is unable to serve his or her country anymore, or an athlete who can no longer play and they aren't a part of a certain group anymore. I'll be honest, playing football was a very effective way to vent my stress, anger, and pain. It was a legal way to get into a fight, kick someone's butt, and not have to go to jail for it. But, when you're not playing anymore, what do you do with all that aggression and negative energy? I know from personal experience that those feelings are still there. They don't go away.

When you become successful, other people may get on the bandwagon or adopt the mind-set of, *Well, my son, my daughter, (or cousin) is successful, so now I can quit.* Successful people want to keep going, regardless of where they are, but an unsuccessful mind-set wants to stop at the first opportunity or chance they get to kick of their shoes and watch someone else do all the work while they reap the benefits. Please know that I want the best for you and your family—whether you're the parent or the child. For this to happen, it's important to develop a mind-set of continual growth and new goals. You and I were born to tackle challenges and achieve great things. We weren't wired to be settlers.

## Setbacks

A setback is basically just a setup for a breakthrough. Setbacks weren't designed or intended to cause us to experience a breakdown. Instead, setbacks are intended to help break us free. At Florida State, I was hoping to be drafted as a first-round pick, but I ended up being selected in the third round. I was very depressed and disappointed in myself. I set a higher standard for myself. I felt like I'd not only let myself down but my entire family as well. It wasn't how my dream as a child went. I was supposed to come out of college the same way I came out of high school, as a consensus All-American and the number-one rated safety in the country, which would've solidified me as a first-round draft pick. I dreamed of being invited to the NFL draft in New York City, and I envisioned my family joining me on stage after the NFL Commissioner called my name. Oh well, I can't go back and change that one.

But, being drafted by the Pittsburgh Steelers in the third

round ended up being a big blessing for me. In fact, looking back, it was the best thing that happened to me in my entire professional career. To have the opportunity to play for the best NFL franchise, maybe the best in all of sports, and to be blessed to be around so many quality individuals and to learn how to become a professional from them was a gift in itself. John Mason, a best-selling author, minister, and, most importantly, friend, once shared with me, "What you learn on your path to your goals is actually more valuable than achieving the goal itself." One of my main ambitions as an athlete on the professional level was to be recognized as the best or one of the best at my position, which is no different than I'd been on every other level of football I've ever played. This didn't happen overnight for me. But, the anger, disappointment, and frustration from not being a first-round pick was the fuel I needed to strain and push myself to get to where I always knew I should've been from the very beginning—the top of the list at my position. Setbacks often reveal the need to improve. Despite all the things that have happened to me, I've always used that humbling draft pick as my motivation.

## Fight for Every Inch

Earlier, I shared with you how in most all sports, but specifically football, the margin of error is so small. One half-step too late or too early results in you not being able to be at the spot where you're needed most. I mean this literally. It can come down to actual inches or seconds. I know the words inches and seconds sound so insignificant, but that hidden yardage or loss of time will be the difference between winning or losing a game. We must always be alert and stay aware, because the inches we need are all around us. However, the most important inches are the six inches between our two ears.

The other side of fighting for inches isn't to let small challenges become huge adversities. Instead, deal with the issue when it's small. This is one of my worst character traits. When it comes to looking a small problem in the eye and facing it, I normally run or put it off until it becomes terminal, which is very similar to the snowball effect. Wikipedia defines the snowball effect as "the process that starts from an initial state of small significance and builds upon itself, becoming larger . . . and also perhaps potentially dangerous or disastrous."

Sooner or later, the same rug you keep sweeping things under will be the same rug you either trip over or get snatched out from underneath you. Having a tough conversation may be an inconvenience, but it doesn't mean it won't be conducive to something better. Talk out problems in the beginning and don't wait. This will immediately open the door for solutions instead of arguments.

## Hold On to Promises

The best way to stay mentally and spiritually strong through adversity is to hold on to something stronger than you are. God has never made me a promise that was too good to be true. My junior year in high school, my Aunt Adlene gave me a book of Bible promises, filled with verses on belief, courage, faith, guidance, hope, patience, prayer, strength, and more. I read that little book before every game and before every practice—from the moment she gave it to me in high school through college and throughout my entire NFL career. I still have that book to this day. The blue leather cover is worn, and the gold lettering is almost completely faded off. But, those promises are still imprinted in my heart. Even after retiring from football, I'd find myself referring to that book whenever I needed a word of encouragement or direction about a decision or problem I'm facing.

Without knowing and holding on to God's good intentions toward me, I wouldn't have persevered through the many trials I'd faced and still achieved my goals. And that's still true in the goals my wife and I have for our family's future. Do you know that God is also with you? Do you know that He hears and sees you? And do you know, deep in your heart that He loves you?

As Hebrews 13:5-6 states, "For He Himself has said, 'I will never leave you nor forsake you.' So, we may boldly say: "The Lord is my helper; I will not fear. What can man do to me?"

One of my favorite Bible verses of all time is found in James 1:2-4. It says, "Consider it pure joy my brother, whenever you face trials of many kinds, because you know the testing of your faith develops perseverance. Perseverance must continue its work so that you may be mature and complete, not lacking anything." We're not alone in the struggle.

## Don't Try to Tackle Adversity Alone

So many of us want *presents* from God, but we don't desire His *presence* in our lives. When I first moved to Nashville to play with the Titans, I had what I call a "Google" relationship with God. *What is that?* I'm glad you asked. I knew who God was. I knew He was still there, and I knew how to pray. I also knew I could ask Him for things, but I didn't have a personal relationship with Him. It was very similar to how fans can Google me or any other athlete or celebrity and find out all types of important and personal information about us. After accumulating all the detailed information from the articles they've researched, they could easily persuade others that they really knew us. But Google relationships don't really let you know who we are as people. In my situation, it was more like I knew God was way up in the stands looking at me, but I wasn't sure if He was getting all my messages or if He still cared about me the same way He used to.

The truth is, God wants to help you not only set goals, He also wants to help you achieve your goals, especially when they line up with His purpose for your life. Even more, He wants to have a fatherly, everyday, loving, relationship with you.

Growing up, I had some older cousins and friends who already had children, but they didn't live in the same house together. So, before I had kids of my own, I'd ask them if parenting was tough. They all responded the same way: "It's not as difficult as everyone makes it seem." Edward De Bono summed up their responses perfectly when he said, "Perception is real even when it is not reality." Now that I'm a father of two beautiful children, I realize the best thing we can invest in our children is our time. The world doesn't have any more job openings for part-time dads or moms. Being a parent is both a full-time and a lifetime gig. I can really understand the importance of this and witness the positive effects of having both parents present in the home. The personal relationship and friendship you develop is like no other. The bond you build by interacting and conversing with one another daily is paramount to how much you can understand and unconditionally love someone.

"Don't worry that children never listen to you; worry that they are always watching you," says Robert Fulghum. This reminds me of an old saying that states, "Children are good imitators, so we as parents must give them something great to imitate." There's nothing wrong with being a copycat, as long as you're copying the right cat. In John 10:27-28, Jesus says, "My sheep hear my voice, and I know them, and they follow me." I can relate to that, because I can be in the loudest Chuck E. Cheese's in the world, and if my son or daughter cries out for me, I'll come running, because I know their voices.

# How Do You Know Your Purpose?

No matter what battles we face, understand that many of them are attacks on your God-given purpose. Bishop Walker says it all the time: "The devil isn't always specifically after you or me. He is more concerned or in pursuit of stopping us from accomplishing and fulfilling our assignment, which has a far greater impact and influence on the world."

Your purpose, your passion, is worth fighting for. I define purpose as something you love doing and would do it without asking for a dime. You might have many different gifts and abilities, but there are things you genuinely love doing—and a paycheck isn't the motivation. Whatever you're most passionate about is what God will assign you to do. Your heart has to be in it and not just your head. Matthew 6:21 and Luke 12:34 both say, "For where your treasure is, there your heart will be also."

For me, football was a gift from God. It helped pave the way for me to fulfill my purpose in life. I think my passion is helping people. My purpose is way beyond sports, but sports was one way I could connect with people, help them, and use the stage and fan base that football afforded me. God still blesses every one of us with gifts and talents, but we, individually, must fight for our purpose. Bishop Walker once said, "The person who has the cure for cancer might be locked up in prison right now." How tragic is a life unfulfilled and a talent misapplied? It's like a drug dealer who runs a multilevel drug organization. He could use that same skill set and be a CEO of a Fortune 500 company, but he didn't fight for his real purpose in life.

## Fighting Limitations

In a chapel I attended in January of 2001 right before my last game as a Florida State Seminole, the team chaplain spoke about the challenge of the four limitations we all face in life. These are:

1. The limitation of time: No one lives on this Earth forever.
2. The limitation of our gifts: No one can do it all.
3. The limitation of our resources: No one can have it all.
4. The limitation of our relationships: No one can please everybody.

I must grudgingly agree with the chaplain. We all have limitations, and these four are important to keep in mind as we set goals and tackle adversities in our own lives. We don't live forever, so let's get on with what really matters—with people who really matter to us. We can't do it all, but we can all do something. So, why not do something that is in line with the purpose that God placed in you? There's an old saying I like that goes, "All gave some, some gave all." When it's all said and done, which one will you be?

We can't have it all, but we have more abilities and resources than we know. The key is to decide to move forward. Jim Rohn, entrepreneur, author, and motivational speaker, said, "The 'why' comes first then the 'how.'" God will supply along the way. We can't please everyone. So, stop trying.

## Painful Reminders

Sure, in the end, you might have some scars from battle. Good for you. I've been told, "Scars are tattoos with better stories." My shoulder still hurts from tackling The Bus, but I wouldn't trade that memory for the world. In the end, it's about looking back on the battles without regrets. When you tackle adversities, you not only become the person you were designed to be, you'll also be an example to your friends and family. Ironically, the most painful memories we all will one day have are those times we gave up or gave in.

Don't.

## TURNOVERS

- We can't have "big" if "little" has us. When "little" has us, we become comfortable and complacent with our current situations, and we stop setting goals for ourselves. We also stop dreaming and fighting for the desires of our hearts.

- Don't waste valuable time crying and complaining over the "what if's" instead of focusing on "what is." Being depressed, beating yourself up, or worrying over things you can't go back and change is useless. As John Mason says, "Worrying is interest paid in advance on something you may never own."

- Don't let small issues grow into big problems. Ignoring our problems doesn't fix them—it only makes them grow bigger and stay longer.

## TAKEAWAYS

- Sometimes less is more. There is a verse in the book of Proverbs that reminds us that "it's better to have less with peace, than a lot with trouble."

- All bad decisions aren't permanent. Keep your focus and your faith when facing adversity. If you remain persistent, everything will work out in your favor, and good things will happen for you and to you.

- Fear is temporary, but regret is forever. Being afraid to lose is being human, but being scared to try is being a coward. Trying is failing at something with honor.

# Chapter 17

# YOUR SUPER BOWL

What's your vision for the future? Do you not want to witness the divine seed that was placed inside of you? The key ingredients to achieve success are the direct results of effective goal setting. A vision without action is just a daydream, and action without a vision is a nightmare. Like any other dreams we have, when our dreams begin to become nightmares, it's time for us to wake up. And I suggest you do it quickly.

Before we start writing out our bucket lists for life, we must first be sure that we have a big enough bucket. You'll find that achievements are made easy when your outer goals become inner commitments. If you can't see the mark, I can guarantee that you won't be able to press toward it, let alone hit it. In my mind, the word Bible is an acronym for "Basic Instructions Before Leaving Earth." The Bible was created for us to see and understand God's vision for our lives. Without a clear vision for your life, what will the dash between your birthdate and death date signify?

We all need a big vision. Remember, the bigger your vision, the bigger your God. In fact, King Solomon said in Proverbs 29:18, "Where there is no vision, the people perish." He's basically saying that if you don't have a vision, then you don't truly know where you're going. If this applies to you, I'd be terrified right about now. I mean, would you go to the airport and board a plane without knowing the plane's final destination? As Helen Keller said, "The only thing worse than being blind is having sight and no vision."

We each need to act on our vision. Some people have huge dreams, but they take no action. Others are super busy, but don't have a strong vision to focus their action. The goal is not to stay busy but to stay progressive. Progress is what keeps us alive. Busyness produces activity; whereas, progressiveness produces accomplishments. We wait on God to move, but He's waiting for us to act. Don't step out on presumption. Instead, step out on permission. When God gives you permission, He will also give you the power. As Bishop Walker says, "There can be no divine intervention without human responsibility." As stated in James 2:12 (KJV), "Faith without works is dead." In other words, once we learn to master our inner worlds, mastering the outside world will be easy.

When I was planning my course to the NFL, Pro Bowl, and Super Bowl, I had to give God my plans. While I planned the course, God directed my steps. I wanted to be drafted in the first round, but I was drafted in the third round. I shared my disappointments on my draft day earlier, but, regardless, I was still in the National Football League. I wanted to make the Pro Bowl as a Pittsburgh Steeler, so Troy Polamalu and I could go to Hawaii as the starting safeties in the Pro Bowl from the same team. However, it didn't happen like I planned. I ended up having to meet him in Hawaii as a representative of the Tennessee Titans. For a consolation prize, we still ended up starting side-by-side in the game, for one last time in our careers.

I share this because even if you write down your vision, it doesn't mean it will go according to your plan and that everything you write down will automatically happen in your life. It just means your commitment to achieving your goals will naturally flow parallel with the thoughts that help shape your vision. Seeing your goal written down will have a powerful effect on your mind. If you can't write it down, then you won't be able to read it. And, if you can't read it, you won't be able to run after it or run with it.

## The Hammer

Even though most people call me Chris, my full first name is Christopher. With that said, you probably didn't know I was named after my grandma, whose name was Christine. You might even know that my nickname is The Hammer, but you'll never guess the real story behind that name. Let's just say the name, Hammer, wasn't something I happily embraced in the beginning.

One day, when I was about seven years old, I was running around playing in the yard with some of my older cousins, when suddenly my two uncles, Charles and Will, started laughing at and joking on me. "Boy, when is your body going to catch up with that big head of yours? You have a hook on the back of your head shaped like a hammer!" Boy, was I steaming hot. Everyone started picking, pointing, and laughing at me. I think I may have even run home crying, because I was so ashamed, mad, and hurt.

So, from that day forward, my uncles and the rest of my family, started calling me Hammer. To say I didn't like it at first would be an understatement, but I've always had the ability to take what happens to me and to use it as motivation. It's amazing how strategic God is with his timing. This all happened during the summer right before football practice started. One of the downsides of coming from a small town is that news travels across town pretty fast. So, kids, not just in my neighborhood but all around town, started calling me Hammer also. My Uncle Charles' youngest son Kelvin, who is one year older than I am, played on the same football team with me. I'll never forget our first live scrimmage against another team. My dad, brother, and uncle came to watch us play. Before the game started, as I ran onto the field, I heard my Uncle Charles yell from the sideline "Put that hammer on 'em Hamma!"

That is when I grew into the name. My body still hadn't quite caught up with my head, but I began to like it. It was pretty cool to have kids around town that I didn't know come up to me and call me Hammer. To this day, when I go back home to Rock Hill, some of my uncles, cousins, and childhood friends refer to me as Hammer. My college and NFL teammates knew my nickname was Hammer, but it faded away as I got older (or, should I say, the rest of my body finally caught up with my head). When I would make a big hit during a game, they would occasionally refer back to it, but it never stuck like it did back when I was growing up.

If you're going to let people ridicule you and call you a name like Hammer, make it your mission to live up to your name and hammer out your goals. But first, make sure you have the right goals. Yeah, I was able to accomplish a grocery list of awesome goals like winning a National Championship, being drafted, and winning the Super Bowl. But I didn't have peace. Honestly, I didn't know peace was available and didn't realize how some of my own choices were keeping me from it.

In fact, for a long time, I considered myself a huge failure for not being able to influence the mind-sets of my closest family members. Consequently, I went through a deep depression for quite some time, because I couldn't understand how I did such a great job of reprogramming the mind-sets of so many of my teammates and friends, but I couldn't transform the mind-sets of the people who mattered the most. Thankfully, I started to question myself and to ask for help.

## Ask

You can't say you want to be a millionaire if you've never asked to be a millionaire. It's just not going to happen. That's because you must speak it into existence. Don't tell me you want to enjoy your family, if you don't ask God to help you fight for peace within your family. Life will pay you whatever you ask of it.

As a kid growing up, and even when I was playing in the NFL, I never dreamed of being a Hall of Famer. I never envisioned myself up on the stage in Canton, Ohio, giving my induction speech. And guess what? I won't be getting fitted for my yellow jacket anytime soon. Oprah Winfrey believes that "we get in life what we have the courage to ask for."

As I mentioned in a previous chapter, one of my most important practices in life is finding people who have mastered the things I aspire to learn to do and then asking them to teach me how to do it. I'm not too prideful to ask for help or to admit I don't have all the answers. Sure, there are certain people you'll meet in life who aren't open books and may not be willing to help you. Don't take it personally. Just move on and avoid wasting your time on those people.

There will also be some people you meet in life who are willing to only teach you everything you know, but not everything they know. But, if you're fortunate like myself, you will also come across people in your life who are willing to teach you everything they know. There's a big difference between the two. I was blessed to know and befriend many of these good people during my NFL career. And some of these mentors were also my biggest competitors. Imagine that. They were competing against me for the top positions within our team, but they helped me anyway. So, don't be afraid to ask for what you're working toward. Instead, be afraid *not* to ask. Expect God to answer and be ready to act.

## New Dreams

You're always changing and growing, and life always throws you new challenges and opportunities. In fact, life is a lot like the ocean. Some days will be calm and still; whereas, other days will be rough and bumpy. But, if you're totally committed, no matter what the conditions are, you'll learn to just ride the waves. No two days will ever be the same, which means we can't afford to stay the same either. The minute you stop dreaming and become complacent is the day you stop living.

Many of us believe just because we are working hard at something, it automatically means we are living our lives to the fullest or making a difference. When, in all actuality, what we're doing is very similar to running on a treadmill or walking up a StairMaster. No matter how hard we're working by jogging, running, or walking—on the fastest speed or the highest incline—we're still not going anywhere. There's a lot of movement, but no motion. As a matter of fact, you're going nowhere; you're just doing it fast.

When people read, "wearenowhere," there will be some who see "we are now *here*;" whereas, others will see "we are *nowhere*." It's all about mind-set and perception. One thing that comes to mind that is stationary but travels all around the world is a postage stamp. Its usefulness is connected to sticking to something until it arrives at its final destination. Let's be honest. All our purposes in life are more valuable than a postage stamp. So, there's no harm in staying committed to your assignment, just make sure that you are being progressive and that you don't become stagnant.

## Everything God Wants You to Be

You can't consider yourself a true professional if you slack off or perform poorly in numerous areas of your life. My definition of a true professional is someone who's professional in everything they do. Cutting corners isn't in their DNA. Why be a great athlete and a terrible student? Why be a successful CEO and a terrible dad?

I'm a true professional. That means I dress professionally, I talk professionally, and I act professionally. If my goal is to be great, it never stops. I'm pursuing impact and success, which translates into significance. It's not money I'm after. You could have millions in the bank but still work. That's what I admired the most about my grandfather (who didn't have millions by the way), and about a lot of the wealthy people I've met over the years. They all share the same mentality—that if a man doesn't work, he doesn't eat. If you cut the engine off, it's hard to turn it back on. So, never turn the engine completely off. To be honest, I'm afraid to put my life in neutral, so I always stay on the throttle.

Confidence is easy to lose and hard to gain. So are money, success, trust, and peace. The same energy, passion, and determination I brought to my sports career is what I've brought to my other pursuits since I retired. It's the same energy I want to pour into people—being a husband and dad, writing this book, being a speaker, and a businessman. As a kid, I gave myself permission to dream, but once I became financially successful, all the drama made it seem unfair and selfish to dream bigger. Not anymore. Dreaming big isn't setting yourself up for failure. Instead, it's setting God up for a miracle.

When I trained and prepared for the upcoming season, I always worked out with guys who were faster and stronger than I was, because it made me better. It pushed me and conditioned me to always give maximum effort. Today, I have a group of mentors who are older than me—and more financially successful. I meet with them once or twice a week. They're not only teaching me how to grow my wealth, but also what not to do as well as what to look out for. When I retired from playing football, I asked God to connect me with the All-Stars of the business world.

Within a few months, through some unexpected connections, I was invited to an event. Of the 40 people there, I was the youngest, probably the least well-off, and the only black man in the room. And, most importantly, I met everyone I'd prayed to God about. That's right: Everyone I wanted to meet was at that one event. It was pretty much the "Who's Who" of Nashville. I got out of my comfort zone, humbled myself, and I asked lots of questions and requested their business cards. Since then, I've built some of the best relationships and true friendships with many of the men I met that night. For me, I found that an hour with one of these wise men could be more valuable than a college degree.

It's important to talk about your dreams and to release them into the atmosphere. However, be careful about sharing your dreams with everybody. Only share your dreams with those you truly trust. And don't ask other people to make your dreams come true. You make your own dreams come true. Never dream or hope for it more than you are willing to work for.

As an athlete, all I ever wanted from my coach was a chance. I'd often think, "*Just put me in the game, Coach. You don't have to make the play for me. Just put me in the game so I can make the play myself!*" You must be careful about what you ask for, because, when you least expect it, God will give it to you, and you must be prepared for it. It's better to be prepared for an opportunity and not have one, than to have an opportunity and not be prepared. I prayed for this moment, and now it's time to put up or shut up. I want everything that God has for me, and I don't want anything that He doesn't want me to have.

## True Riches

There are plenty of people who have a lot of money, but no friends. There are many people who have millions of dollars, but no peace within their family. The success I'm talking about is to enjoy healthy, loving relationships. In 1 Timothy 6:6, the apostle Paul said to a young man he was mentoring, "Godliness with contentment is great gain." And legendary Reggae singer Bob Marley said, "I'm not rich in possessions or money, but my riches are in life forever." Marley understood that it was more important to make an impact instead of an income. And Chuck Palahniuk said, "The goal isn't to live forever but to create something that will."

We need to stop focusing so much on making a living and start focusing on designing the life we want for ourselves. We must not be afraid to dream. We must be willing to ask. And we must be prepared to fight. Our destiny depends on it.

I read this article in *The Huffington Post* titled, "The Power of Knowing Your Purpose," which was written by Megan Tull. In it she says, "The purpose of life is to discover your gift. The work of life is to develop it. The meaning of life is to give your gift away." And Tenzin Gyatso, the 14th Dalai Lama, says, "Share your knowledge. It's a way to achieve mortality."

These quotes sum up the circle of life to me. They explain the true reasoning behind our existence in this world. We've all been uniquely created and designed to complete this massive-sized puzzle, but we're the only ones with the pieces that can fit our spaces. To complete our assignments in the allotted time here on Earth, we must dream our dream, ask the right questions, and then fight for our lives to place our piece of the puzzle in its respective place. There is an old saying, "Don't go where the path may lead you, go to where there is no path and leave a trail."

## It's Not Too Late

It's not too late to dream, ask, and grow. It's not too late to say "no." You're the quarterback of your life, and you don't have to run the play you originally called in the huddle. You have the power to call an audible at the line of scrimmage and change the entire direction of the game. In the beginning, your positive change might be painful for you, and for some friends and family, but, in the long run, it will be better for everybody. That's because every lesson not truly learned will be repeated. Unfortunately, I had to stop talking to some of the closest people in my life who didn't respect the healthy boundaries I started to set for myself. But I never stopped praying for them.

The first step is having a vision of what true success looks like for you. I like the saying, "If you can't see it before you see it, then you will never see it." You must understand the issues causing the drama and strife in your life and identify how you've played a part in the unhealthy relationships. Then, you must reprogram your mind to love people and use things, not the other way around.

## For Parents

If you're a parent of a successful child—a CEO, doctor, professional athlete, or a standout elementary school student—I hope you know that my heart goes out to you, and all parents. I want you to enjoy a good life and a wonderful relationship with your kids. To begin this journey, ask yourself some tough questions:

- What am I doing too much of? Am I too involved in their life? Are my expectations fair?
- Am I relying on my child to be my provider—even if they're young? And by doing so, have I abandoned my God-given dreams?
- Is there something I, as the parent, missed as a child that I'm now trying to live or regain through my kids? Am I using my child's success to feed my own ego?
- What happens if my child doesn't make it? What happens if I invest a lot of time and money in my kid's

pursuit and they quit?

- Am I doing this for my child, or for me? Have I strong-armed my child's life and dreams?

Don't take advantage of your kids, take advantage of the opportunities they provide you. Learn how to empower people and not enable, or be enabled by, them. And when that day comes to where you must rely on a child or particularly a son, make sure it's the Son of Man you put all your faith and trust in, not your own son! Jesus is the only one who can truly save you.

## Receive

Asking is acknowledging that you're not alone in this game of life. God relied on own His Son to come down from Heaven to carry out His assignment and save the world from sin. And now, God relies on His children—us—to live out the assignment He has for us. Even Jesus had some hesitation about carrying out the assignment God planned for Him. Can you imagine the heaviness in God's heart when He placed the burden of death on His own son? Ultimately, Jesus put His trust in God, and we must also follow His example if we want to be empowered.

## To You as the Child

As a child, our biggest role models are our parents. But they're human, and they'll be the first to admit to that fact. Regardless of how all-knowing and all-powerful they make us feel as kids, they don't know all the answers. So, stop complaining about what your parents can't do, couldn't do, or didn't do for you. They are giving you all they have and telling you all they know. I can assure you they are making the best decisions for you and the rest of the family where they are in their lives right now.

Instead, the questions I want you to ask yourself are, "Where did these wrong expectations come from? Who or what planted these seeds in your spirit?" Where did the mind-set of, "Mom, Dad, I made it—now you can retire!" come from? And, when did it become normal to recruit a personal entourage from your friends and family, and put them on your payroll, just because you share the same last name, or you grew up in the same neighborhood?

The Bible says that you'll know good people, and good ideas, from their "fruit." In other words, if what you're saying "yes" and "no" to is working, great. Keep up the good work. But if there is chaos, strife, and heartache, maybe it's time to rethink and reset your boundaries and to come up with a new game plan.

## A Vision of Peace

The 2006 Super Bowl was the highlight of my career, but not the highlight of my life. Honestly, every day that I wake up with love for my family and peace in my heart is the best day of my life. I had to learn how to let go and let God. When I tried to fix my life in terms of my relationships with my family and close friends, the problems faded away briefly but always resurfaced. However, when God deals with our situations, our problems are gone and never return.

I want this to be true for you, too. This is your time. This is your Super Bowl.

*Hammer away.*

# EXPECTATIONS

## Parents

Following are some healthy expectations parents have for their children:

- To listen to them and obey their rules
- To be successful at life due to the solid foundation they have set as parents
- To be leaders
- To be independent
- To know how to survive (e.g., cook, clean, laundry)
- To make good choices and decisions
- To speak up and use their voices
- To not let people take advantage of them
- To protect/defend themselves

- To be confident
- To be well-mannered
- To be well-spoken
- To make their parents proud
- To honor and add value to their family name (i.e. not to embarrass their name)
- To be kind and respectful to others
- To stay out of trouble (i.e. jail)
- To do their assigned chores
- To be good citizens
- To believe in God
- To be good students
- To graduate from high school/college
- To not become a parent while still living under their roof
- To not be late for curfew
- To not have any speeding tickets or car accidents
- To not abuse drugs or alcohol
- To select good friends
- To go farther than they went as kids
- To be there for them when they get older and can't take care of themselves anymore (i.e. hospital visits, doctor's appointments, baths, feeding them, bringing the grand-kids over to visit them, transportation to church, stopping by just to spend time and talk with them)
- To not let them die lonely in a retirement home
- To bury them when they die

- To carry out their will and testament

Following are some unhealthy expectations parents have for their children:

- To automatically assume their children will take care of them because of what they provided for their kids when they were younger
- To think that their child will take care of them forever
- To retire them from their jobs
- To get a job and pay all/some of their bills
- That if you hold your child back or start them late in school, you will give them a competitive edge in the classroom and on the field of sports
- To not only get married, but to marry the person of their liking
- To make them grandparents
- To buy them a house or pay off their current home
- To buy them a new car
- To pay off all their debts
- To allow them to live out all their childhood dreams and fantasies.
- To make up or repay them for all the sacrifices they made
- To take over the family business
- To follow in the same career path or work in the same

field (i.e. doctor, coach, athlete, lawyer, dentist, teacher, pastor)

- To not only go to college, but go to the same college they attended
- To offer financial, emotional, and physical support when needed
- To always put them first over their child's spouses
- To be moved into their child's home when they get older
- To pay for them to live in a retirement home

## The World

Following are some unhealthy expectations the world tries to place on us:

- To retire and buy our parents a new home
- To give back and pour out into our communities
- To be big givers to charities, churches, and to the less fortunate
- To think that successful people owe a debt to the churches, communities, cities, schools, and organizations that helped them
- To feel pressured to marry someone because of obligation instead of true love (e.g., dating them for a long time, being with them before you became rich, marrying someone because they are rich, marrying them because

of a position they hold, profession their in, power they possess, or due to having pre-existing children together)

- To have expectations based upon where a person is born as to whether or not they are suppose to make it out and become successful (i.e. poverty, skin color, education)
- To believe that sports and entertainment are the only way out for people of color
- To think all professional athletes are rich
- To think athletes get all the money in their contracts
- To think athletes have no emotions or feelings
- To think people with money have no problems
- To think that all athletes are dumb jocks with lots of money
- To think that all rich people are snobby and arrogant
- To think that all rich people are big spenders who don't value careful spending
- To think all successful people love what they do
- To be pressured and influenced by their co-workers and friends to quit their jobs, as a result of their kids becoming successful

## Successful People

Following are some erroneous expectations many successful people are tempted to believe:

- Everyone wants something from us.
- We can help and save everyone.
- We have unlimited resources.
- No one can be trusted.
- Everyone should give us first-class treatment.
- People should trust and follow us, because we are successful.
- Just because we are successful, we can change or motivate everyone.
- People who aren't or haven't been as successful as we are, can't bring us any value.
- We should openly trust our financial advisors, agents, publicists, family members, and the people closet to us to handle all our business affairs while we just focus on the money-making part.
- When we expect those closest to us to have the same dreams that we have.
- We think those closest to us want the same things out of life that we want.
- We think that everyone is wired like us.
- We think that money is the answer to everything.
- We think money can buy us happiness.
- We think money can buy us out of trouble or every situation we get in.
- We think that everyone will automatically like us just because we are successful.

- We think we will never run out of money.

- We think we are above the law.

- We think we are invincible and indestructible.

- We think we don't need anyone.

- We think we can do our jobs forever.

- We think we will always make the same amount of money our entire lives.

- We think that everyone in our crowd is in our corner.

## Avoiding Turnovers

And lastly, the following should help as you work to avoid turnovers in your life:

- Don't "retire" your parents from their jobs. Instead, encourage them to work an easier job, depending on how old they are.

- Don't shower your family members and others with gifts and trips—pay off their debts first.

- Don't encourage your family members to not work at all. It will only lead to resentment and anger when you're the only one working hard and providing, while everyone else is resting, relaxing, and watching you, but calling all the shots.

- Use your influence and your connections to get your loved ones a better job with less physical demands on their bodies, or possibly help them get their dream job.

- Don't put your parents on an allowance, because it will change the dynamics of your relationship with them, as you will become their parent.

- Don't just freely give to your family all the time. Invest in your family. Make them earn it and give them incentives.

- Don't automatically trust that your family will do right with the money you assist them with. In most cases, having access to a lot of money is new to everyone in the family.

- Encourage the entire family to take a financial class. (I recommend the course titled "Financial Peace" by Dave Ramsey.)

- Don't say yes, every time they ask you for something.

- Keep them honest and make them put some "skin in the game."

- Don't start off paying for every food bill, airline ticket, and hotel stay when they come to visit you. That's how the expectation monster is birthed. Just like dating, how you start off is how they expect you to finish.

- Before hand, give whomever you would like to bless some money, so they can pull it out when the bill comes as if they are paying with their own money.

- Lend only what you can comfortably afford to give or lose, and don't get upset if you don't get it back.

- Don't spoil your family so soon. You had to work hard and show yourself worthy to your employer before they wrote you a big check. Make them do the same.

- Make your family put all their debts, student loans, credit cards, outstanding balances, etc. on the table upfront.

- Until their debts are paid in full, don't spend large amounts of money on your family.

- Preach, encourage, and motivate your family to become debt free.

- Don't allow your family to use your celebrity/connections to help them do less, be lazy, or take advantage of people.

- Don't give cash. When asked to pay a bill, ask to see the actual invoice.

- Don't buy them what's applaudable. Instead, buy them what's affordable and maintainable.

- Don't get caught making emotional decisions.

- Always spend some time in prayer before you make a big decision.

- Don't try to repay your parents and those who have helped/sacrificed for you with gifts and money. It will never be enough.

- And don't cosign for anyone. If they end up being unable to pay off their debt, it will become yours. And some may even go into the contract thinking you owe them anyway, so they won't be that dedicated to honoring their end of the agreement to begin with.

- Always count the cost. Think about the ending at the beginning.

- Don't sign a lifetime contract to take care of someone, when your contract isn't a lifetime deal.

- Don't make yourself responsible for someone else's dreams and expectations.

- Don't make promises or take over someone else's debt. People seem to hold you more accountable for what you say you will do for them than what they commit to doing for themselves.

- Get to know everyone's infamous unknown uncle, Uncle Sam.

- Make everyone start off with a credit score of zero with you. Then, make them earn their score—and your trust.

- Make sure you always cut the cards/deck.

- People don't ask you to explain your "yes," so don't feel like you must explain your "nos."

- Understand that the same people who are talking bad about you and destroying your reputation, are the same people who at one time or another used to love, worship, and praise you.

- Don't give anyone power of attorney.

- Keep certain things with value (e.g., houses, condos, land, cars) in your name, or keep the title so no one can take a lien out on them to get money.